BIG TRUTH LITTLE BOOKS™

WHAT THE BIBLE SAYS ABOUT HOSPITALITY

Cliff McManis

With All Wisdom Publications
Cupertino, California

WHAT THE BIBLE SAYS ABOUT HOSPITALITY

What the Bible Says About Hospitality
Copyright © 2019 Cliff McManis
Published by WITH ALL WISDOM PUBLICATIONS
Requests for information about **BIG TRUTH** LITTLE BOOKS® can be
sent to:

Publications@creeksidebiblechurch.com

All Scripture quotations unless otherwise noted, or from the
New American Standard Bible. © Copyright 1960, 1962, 1963,
1968, 1971, 1972, 1973, 1975, 1977, 1995 by the Lockman
Foundation. Used by permission.

What the Bible Says About Hospitality is volume 13 in the Big Truth
little books® series.

General Editor: Cliff McManis
Series Editor: Derek Brown
Associate Editors: J. R. Cuevas, Breanna Paniagua, Jasmine Patton
Proofreader: Sergio Gonzalez
Cover Design: Oluwasanya Awe

CONTENTS

SERIES PREFACE

Our mission with the *BIG TRUTH little books*® series is to provide edifying, accessible literature for Christian readers from all walks of life. We understand that it is often difficult to find time to read good books. But we also understand that reading is a valuable means of spiritual growth. The answer? Get some really big truth into some little books. These books may be small, but each is full of Scripture, theological reflection, and pastoral insight. Our hope is that Christians young and old will benefit from these books as they grow in their knowledge of Christ through His Word.

Cliff McManis, General Editor
Derek Brown, Series Editor

INTRODUCTION

"Love ye…the stranger…" (Deut 10:19, KJV)

When you hear the word "hospitality" what is the first thing that comes to mind? Do you think of Oprah, the most high-profile philanthropist of our day? Or maybe Martha Stewart, the popular and inveterate specialist on all things "entertaining"? Many think of the Catholic nun, Mother Theresa, the incomparable modern model of one who cared for others selflessly and constantly. Or, maybe your thoughts raced in some other direction.

"Hospitality," or the idea of welcoming a stranger into the community by meeting practical needs like food and shelter, has been a common practice by many social groups all over the world since ancient times. The Bible, however, elevates this practice with higher spiritual and theological nuances, with greater implications regarding the roles of the host and the guest by virtue of God's role as the ultimate Host throughout history, and Christ's role as both Host and Guest during the course of His earthly ministry. So biblical hospitality is distinctly set apart and completely unique compared to all other forms and definitions of hospitality. The goal of this little book is to show why that is the case.

Christians are commanded to practice hospitality. Scripture clearly exhorts believers to be "practicing hospitality" (Rom 12:13). But the sad fact is that biblical hospitality is a long lost and forgotten reality in many quarters of the church. Many saints don't practice hospitality. Some professing Christians are not even aware that hospitality is a basic Christian virtue that God expects from all believers. Others think hospitality is optional. A good number think it is primarily or only the task of the professional clergy. Worst of all are the countless Christians who have a faulty understanding of what hospitality is according to the Bible. Many have bought in a worldly and secular counterfeit instead. Hence the need for this little book.

Christians need a fresh reminder from Scripture about the true meaning of biblical hospitality. God has empowered believers with the Holy Spirit to work out their salvation with fear and trembling (Phil 2:12); Christ has saved us to carry out good works toward others (Eph 2:10); believers are obligated to stimulate one another to love and good deeds (Heb 10:24). Regularly practicing the ministry of hospitality is fundamental to what it means to work out our salvation, to do good works, and to stimulate one another toward love and good deeds.

In the future at the final judgment, Christ will judge us based on our works (Rom 2:6-7; 1 Cor 3:13). How we dealt with the divine imperative of "practicing hospitality" will be part of that eternal assessment of our stewardship. For those who were faithful with the holy charge to be hospitable there will be blessing, honor, and reward (Rom 2:7; 1 Cor 3:14). For those who neglected or spurned the call to be hospitable, there will be loss (1 Cor 3:15).

Being hospitable in a biblical manner gives glory to God, exalts Christ, shows dependence on the Spirit, edifies the Church, blesses those in need, and is a tremendous witness to a lost and watching world. In pursuit of these admirable goals we begin with chapter one to establish a biblical definition of hospitality.

1

WHAT IS BIBLICAL HOSPITALITY?

Wrong Views

Many people have crazy notions about what constitutes hospitality. Even Christians have surprisingly odd ideas about it. I remember one church-goer who routinely chided me about the elders of the church not fulfilling their mandate to be hospitable. This person would say unabashedly, "First Timothy three, verse two says elders need to be hospitable. But the elders aren't inviting me to their house for dinner!" This church-goer was serious. Ironically, this impassioned enforcer of New Testament imperatives was not inviting church elders over for dinner either. For this discontented saint, hospitality was a one-way street. As we talked about what hospitality actually means in the Bible, he was adamant that it meant inviting church people over to your house and providing a meal...and it should begin with the elders setting the example. But the simple reality is that hospitality does not mean having your friends over for dinner. That is a misguided and truncated view of what the Bible actually teaches on the matter.

Other Christians have told me that hospitality means going down to the food shelter regularly and handing out cold-cut sandwiches to the poor and homeless. Others propose it is giving a dollar to the guy at the freeway intersection with the cardboard sign, "WILL WORK FOR FOOD." Some Christians restrict hospitality to doing good for unbelievers only. But none of the foregoing actually reflect a complete picture of what the Bible says.

Another popular understanding among Christians is that hospitality is simply having people in your home. That is not a definition of hospitality, but it may be an application of hospitality. If you have a few people in your home for a weekly Bible study, that is not necessarily hospitality—that is a Bible study. If you have friends over for prayer and singing worship songs, that is not hospitality—that is fellowship. If you have several buddies over for the Super Bowl and snacks, that is not hospitality—that's a Super Bowl party.

Another popular but mistaken view of hospitality taught by Christians is the notion that hospitality is one of the spiritual gifts given by the Spirit to certain believers, making a few more suited to employ hospitality than others. This is not true. Hospitality is a mandate God has given to the whole Church collectively and to every Christian individually. If you are a Christian and you are averse to practicing hospitality, it doesn't mean you don't have the gift; rather, it may mean that you are ignorant, have a bad attitude toward this obligation, or simply are holding onto a sinful attitude. All Christians are susceptible here. With regard to spiritual gifts, it is true that there are spiritual gifts (Eph 4:7), and the Spirit does sovereignly distribute the gifts (1 Cor 12:11) to every Christian (12:7). And no Christian has all the gifts (12:29). But hospitality is not a gift; rather, it is a universal ethic, practice, virtue, and obligation. Just as love, prayer, evangelism, discernment, the "one-anothers" and all the other imperatives of the New Testament that are not specialized gifts, but rather commands given by God, so hospitality is a command for all.

In addition to pop Christian renditions of "hospitality" are widespread secular notions. *The English Oxford Dictionary* is typical, which defines "hospitality" as follows: "The friendly and generous reception and entertainment of guests, visitors, or strangers. Relating to or denoting the business of entertaining clients, conference delegates, or other official visitors." The emphasis in this secular definition is on entertainment.

It's from this kind of definition that the chasm grows even wider, distancing the modern understanding of "hospitality" from a biblical notion. Today many universities offer degrees in "hospitality management" which focus on hotel and restaurant management. For example, the Ivy League school, Cornell University in New York, is considered by many to have the best hospitality major in the country. But with this kind of "hospitality" we are far adrift from the biblical mandate of what God meant when He obligated the saints to live hospitable lives.

It is understandable why there is much confusion among Christians over the word "hospitality." The Old Testament was written in Hebrew over 2,500 years ago and the New Testament was written in Greek 2,000 years ago. Yet, our English word "hospitality" is of recent origin finding its derivation from Old French and Medieval Latin.[1] As a result, as is so often the case, much gets lost in translation.

One English dictionary defines hospitality as "friendly treatment of guests." This definition is based on the Latin root which is *hospes* - meaning "guest." This Latin root is the basis of related words like host, hostel, hotel, hospice, hospital (originally meaning "guest house" then over time morphing into "care of the sick").[2] But all these words have a slightly different nuance than the fully-orbed biblical concept. In your modern English Bible, you will find the word "hospitality" only three or four times (cf. NASB, ESV) and the word "hospitable" two times in the New Testament. You won't find the words "hospitable" or "hospitality" at all in your English Old Testament!

Hospitality Means "Stranger-Love"

Why so few references of the word "hospitality" in the Bible? It is because the literal biblical expression for the concept at hand is "stranger-love" not "hospitality." The Bible commands believers to "love strangers." The actual biblical word is picturesque and beautifully descriptive. When I hear the word "hospitable" I think of a big, cold, white hospital building made out of cement and cinder blocks, painted white. When I hear the word "stranger-love" I imagine Christ showing care and concern to an ostracized Samaritan woman alone at a water well. So, with respect to the imperative to be hospitable, the Bible does not call us to be "nice to our friends," but rather to "love strangers." There's a big difference. Scripture is clear and consistent from Genesis through the end of the New Testament in defining hospitality and illustrating it in action. To clear the air on the matter we'll begin by defining hospitality in its biblical context. Then in later chapters we'll consider some representative examples in Scripture.

First Peter 4:9 says, "*Be* hospitable to one another without complaint." In the Greek text here the verb "be" is understood and the word for "hospitable" is the compound word *philoxenoi*. Hiebert offers an excellent definition of this New Testament word, *philoxenoi*: "it describes one who has an affectionate concern for strangers that expresses itself in offering them food and shelter."[3] "Philo" is from the verb *phileo* meaning "love." *Xenos* means "stranger." The fear of strangers,

"Xenophobia," is the opposite of "stranger-love." We could translate the verse above in 1 Peter 4:9 as, "Exhibit stranger-love toward one another." *Phileo* is one of two common words in the New Testament for "love." The word *Philadelphia*, "brotherly love," comes from *phileo* plus *adelphos* which means "brother."

The other common verb in the New Testament for "love" is *agapao* or *agape* the noun. *Phileo* is used about 25 times in the New Testament and *agapao* occurs over 140 times. They are both translated in English as "love," so they are indistinguishable in your average Bible. They are different words, so they do have a nuance of difference in meaning, although they also have some overlap as well. *Agapao* is said to be thoughtful (or volitional) love whereas *phileo* is affection. On occasion the two words seem interchangeable. The immediate context always determines their meaning with each occurrence.

Many have said that *agapao* is God's love—a divine and heavenly love—whereas *phileo* is a finite human love. That is simply false. Jesus said in John 5:20 that "the Father loves the Son." The word for "love" here is *philei*, from *phileo*. *Phileo* is used to speak of God's love. But John 3:35 says, "The Father loves the Son" and in this instance the verb for "love" is *agapao* which also speaks of God's amazing love. Two exact statements in our English Bibles about the Father's love for Christ, both using two different Greek verbs in the original text. This is a good reminder that believers need to beware of shallow word studies and need to remain diligent and discerning, like whenever they might hear a simplistic and overly-dramatic preacher say, "Now people, *agape* is God's unique, supernatural, heavenly love and *phileo* is earthly, human love!"

It is true that most of the time in the New Testament *agapao* refers to good, pure and godly love, but on occasion it refers to ungodly or carnal love. For example, Jesus said wicked people "love" (*agaposin*) each other (Luke 6:32); the evil Pharisees "love" (*agapate*) the front seats in the synagogues (Luke 11:43) and they "loved" (*eigapeisan*) the praise of men (John 12:43); sinners "loved" (*eigapeisan*) the darkness (John 3:19); Paul said all people "love" (*agapan*) themselves (Eph 5:28); Demas the traitor "loved" (*agapeisas*) the present world more than he loved Paul (2 Tim 4:10); and unbelievers "love" this evil world (1 John 2:15). These are examples showing that *agapao* is not reserved for expressing only God's divine love, nor is it a superior word to *phileo* to express love. Each word has its meaning determined by the immediate context in each instance it occurs.

"Stranger-Love" in the New Testament

"Stranger-love," or *philoxenia*, is used five times in the New Testament: three times as a command to all Christians and twice as a requirement for elders.

"Be devoted to one another in brotherly love; give preference to one another in honor, not lagging behind in diligence, fervent in spirit, serving the Lord; rejoicing in hope, persevering in tribulation, devoted to prayer, contributing to the needs of the saints, **practicing hospitality** (*philoxenian*)" (Rom 12:10-13).

"Let love of the brethren continue. Do not neglect to **show hospitality to strangers** (*philoxenios*), for by this some have entertained angels without knowing it. Remember the prisoners, as though in prison with them, and those who are ill-treated, since you yourselves also are in the body" (Heb 13:1-3).

"Above all, keep fervent in your love for one another, because love covers a multitude of sins. **Be hospitable** (*philoxenoi*) to one another without complaint" (1 Pet 4:8-9).

"An overseer, then must be above reproach, the husband of one wife, temperate, prudent, respectable, **hospitable** (*philoxenon*), able to teach, not addicted to wine or pugnacious, but gentle, peaceable, free from the love of money" (1 Tim 3:2-3).

"For the overseer must be above reproach as God's steward, not self-willed, not quick-tempered, not addicted to wine, not pugnacious, not fond of sordid gain, but **hospitable** (*philoxenon*), loving what is good, sensible, just, devout, self-controlled" (Titus 1:7-8).

Practical Observations

Giving some summary observations about how "hospitality" is used in the context of each of the five New Testament passages will help flesh out a complete and practical definition from a biblical perspective. First to note is that being hospitable is a command for all Christians, not just an option. Hey, Christian—stop, pause, and evaluate. When was the last time you practiced "stranger-love"? And how often do you do it? Is it a pattern of your Christian life or a rare occurrence? Or is it non-existent?

Second, in the first three passages mentioned above, the command to be hospitable immediately follows the command to love—specifically "devoted" love, "continual" love, and "fervent" love. The point is clear—if a Christian claims to have the love of Christ, then it will be readily apparent in the way they treat strangers on a regular basis. Spirit-filled, obedient believers will be "devoted" to loving strangers "continually" and "fervently."

Third, the act of hospitality is defined by other commands surrounding it in each passage. Romans 12 says that hospitality won't happen without deliberate "diligence" on the part of believers and it can only happen when you "give preference" to others. People who give preference to themselves, their own convenience, needs, and agenda will not be good at hospitality. Being self-centered is the antithesis to stranger-love. Being preoccupied with self comes naturally to us as sinners and is the American way. However, it undermines this biblical obligation. First Peter says to be hospitable "without complaint." This means helping strangers with food and shelter may inconvenience you, take you out of your routine, drain some of your funds, free time or groceries; invade your personal space; it may get your dishes, your couch or carpet a little dirty—lots of things the average person can "complain" about. If you are a "whiner" then you will have a hard time living out biblical hospitality.

Fourth, the command to love strangers is in the context of living in the Body of Christ. Hebrews 13 is explicit—"Hey, Christian, be hospitable because you yourself are in the Body of Christ." All three passages above are commands given to Christians with respect to how they should treat other believers. Hebrews 13 says plainly to "love the brethren" by being hospitable. The "brethren" is a reference to believers. Romans 12 and 1 Peter 4 say hospitality should be toward "one another"—the one another commands are in reference to fellow Christians. The command to be hospitable is first to be employed and practiced among the needy strangers in the church. This is important to understand because many think the word "stranger" means "unbeliever," but it does not. "Stranger" can mean a believer you don't know. This is exactly what Paul meant when he gave this command to all Christians in Galatians: "So then, while we have opportunity, let us do good to all men, and especially to those who are of the household of the faith" (6:10).

Fifth, hospitality is a requirement for elders as stated by 1 Timothy 3 and Titus 1. In other words, loving strangers is a qualification for being a shepherd. There are over twenty qualifications that should typify the life of a church leader, and welcoming strangers is one of them. In the New Testament an elder is the same thing as a shepherd, pastor, bishop, overseer and presbyter—the words are interchangeable. This does not mean that the elders have to be treating the church members to meals in their homes all the time as the church-goer insisted earlier. That is not biblical "stranger-love." Church members are not "strangers" to local pastors and elders.

As a matter of fact, some church members are a little too familiar with the pastor. The requirement for stranger-love on the part of an elder means that church leaders will have welcoming attitudes toward strangers who frequent their church, especially visiting, unknown believers. And such welcoming attitudes will be backed up with commensurate actions. Why do elders have to be especially faithful to the command of hospitality?

One main reason is because an elder is a shepherd. Pastors must love all the people and be partial to no one. Faithful pastors don't have an option to like some people and not like others. Sadly, some congregants are not held to the same standard—they can pick and choose who they will like, associate with and welcome. This is not the case for the elder, who is an under-shepherd of the Chief-Shepherd, Jesus Christ (1 Pet 5:1-5). Jesus was hospitable to all (including strangers) and partial to none. An elder who does not love people, including strangers, should not be an elder. Sadly, some pastors and churches have had a myopic and exclusionary attitude where they treat foreigners with disinterest, or even contempt.

Wrapping It Up

The goal of this chapter was to simply define biblical hospitality. First it was necessary to expose and dispel the common wrong views. Then define the actual word and concept as found in Scripture; that word is "stranger-love," from the compound Greek word, *philoxenoi*. *Phileo* refers to the love of personal affection and *xenos* means stranger, a person you don't know. We also noted that "strangers" are not unbelievers but fellow believers, as emphasized in the New Testament, who we have not met and who have practical needs.

And since they are members of the Body of Christ, they are fellow spiritual family members, precious children of God, who we need to tend to in light of our relationship with Christ. We also learned that practicing stranger-love is the obligation of every Christian. It is even a special requirement or qualification for elders. Biblical hospitality is showing fervent, welcoming love and affection for fellow believers who are strangers in our midst and have special needs of food, shelter and care by virtue of their transient status.

With the above biblical definition established, let's go on to the next chapter to see Old Testament examples of hospitality among God's people. For it is the Old Testament practice of this special love that set the precedent for the New Testament commands that were entrusted to the Church.

2

HOSPITALITY IN THE OLD TESTAMENT

Moses

New Testament hospitality is a carry-over from Old Testament hospitality. One Bible Dictionary says it best:

> In ancient Israel, hospitality was not merely a question of good manners, but a moral institution which grew out of the harsh desert and nomadic existence led by the people of Israel. The biblical customs of welcoming the weary traveler and of receiving the stranger in one's midst was the matrix out of which hospitality and all its tributary aspects developed into a highly esteemed virtue in Jewish tradition. Biblical law specifically sanctified hospitality toward the 'stranger' who was to be made particularly welcome 'for you were strangers

> in a strange land' (Lev. 19:34; cf. Ex. 12:49).
> Foreign travelers...could count on the
> custom of hospitality.[1]

The command to love strangers flows from the nature of God as revealed from the beginning of Scripture. God has many traits as revealed in Scripture (Exod 34:6-7). One of those traits is love: "God is love" (1 John 4:8). Before his death, Moses reminded the Israelites about their God YHWH, that "Indeed, He loves the people" (Deut 33:3). Humans were made in God's image from the beginning (Gen 1:26-27) and that means God created humans with similar traits that He has, but on a finite, creaturely level. One of those capacities that God gave to humans was the capacity to love. God is a Person; only persons can love. And people have that ability as image-bearers of the Creator. This reality is the basis for God's expectation of believers to love strangers. Because God is love, so we can and must love.

At the end of Jesus' ministry, some Pharisees tried get Him to contradict Himself by asking, "Teacher, which is the great commandment in the Law?" (Matt 22:36). Jesus replied that the two greatest commands included loving God and loving your fellow man. This was not new information. The command to love your neighbor was from the Law of Moses given by God in 1440 BC (Lev 19:18). One's neighbor was any person you came across who was made in God's image. That included strangers.

Jesus reminds us that God's Law is not antithetical to love. As a matter of fact, the theology for stranger-love is codified in the Law of Moses. One key example is from Deuteronomy 10:17-20, when YHWH spoke to Moses in 1400 BC just before the Jews entered the Promised Land. It reads as follows:

> [17] For the LORD your God is the God of gods and the Lord of lords, the great, the mighty, and the awesome God who does not show partiality nor take a bribe. [18] He executes justice for the orphan and the widow, and **shows His love for the alien** by giving him food and clothing. [19] **So show your love for the alien**, for you were aliens in the land of Egypt. [20] You shall fear the LORD your God; you shall serve Him and cling to Him, and you shall swear by His name.

A few key principles on stranger-love flow from this passage. First, in verse 17, Moses reminds the people here that God does not show partiality. Partiality is to show favoritism—to treat one person or group favorably over another for illegitimate reasons, or to treat one group unjustly based on superficial categories. God does not do that. All people are made in His image; therefore, all people are sacred. God does not love one gender more than another, nor adults more than children, nor one social class over another, nor one race over another.

Exemplifying stranger-love begins with this trait of not showing partiality. What is one main reason people are not welcoming to strangers? Because they are partial. Showing favoritism toward our friends comes naturally. We easily gravitate to the familiar and welcome the ones we like while we shy away from the unfamiliar and different. This is why cliques exist in every sizeable social or corporate entity. As bacteria is to our skin, so are cliques to human social life. Having cliques in your church or community is not unique—it's the norm. On occasion, to combat this perennial and ubiquitous conduct of the crowd, well-meaning but naïve micro-managing social engineers in our midst try to squash or disperse the cliques during our various social gatherings through coerced methods. By hoping to force intermingling, they issue threats for not accepting others, and condescendingly look down their nose at a group of teenagers having innocent fun together in the corner. But cliques and partiality cannot be banished from the human heart through external means or contrived manipulation. Partiality can only be held in check by a work of God on the heart as His Spirit awakens us to the true meaning of being other-oriented.

Second, in verse eighteen Moses gives examples of God's impartial love that crosses all barriers, for He loves the unlovable, the down-and-outers that most people typically don't have time for: the orphans, the widows, and the aliens. What do the orphans, widows, and aliens have in common? They have special needs; they need help; they are dependent; their good and their survival is contingent upon the help and intervention of others…and worst of all, they can't give you much in return. Most people just don't want to be bothered or inconvenienced by those prospects.

Moses says God has a special love for "the alien." The NIV Bible translates "alien" here as "foreigner." The King James Bible translates "alien" as "stranger," which is most fitting word, tying in well with the New Testament verses we saw in the last chapter. God is commanding the Israelites that they are obligated to love strangers——they are to give care and affection to people they do not know. They are to employ "stranger-love" or "hospitality." And God gives the reason why His people should love the alien: because God loves the alien! God continues to show His love to strangers by giving them "food and clothing." What does it take to show hospitality to strangers? It takes God-like character, from a negative as well as a positive perspective. The negative is to not be partial. The positive is to be loving as God is loving.

Third, God concludes in verse twenty by telling His people how loving strangers is even possible. It does not come from our own strength, desire, methods or nature. It is possible when we "fear the LORD your God." To fear God is to love God, submit to Him, make Him the priority. To fear God is to obey Him and be willing to be used by Him. To fear God is to acknowledge His holiness, sovereignty, and greatness while seeing our own sin, unworthiness and inadequacy. To fear God is to intimately know God. For us today that means believing in Jesus Christ His Son. Only when we know Christ, can we then have the alien, supernatural power from God to love others more than we love ourselves. God has to change us from the inside out in our very nature before we are able to resist partiality and act in love toward the unfamiliar. Our natural inclination is to love and serve ourselves. So, living out a life of being hospitable begins with the solid foundation of having a right relationship with our Creator through Jesus Christ the Savior.

The Foundation

The quintessential expression of this kind of love for strangers is illustrated in the Old Testament from the life of Abraham who was born around 600 years before Moses. The New Testament showcases Abraham's encounter with three strangers as the premier model of stranger-love that Christians should mimic: "Let love of the brethren continue. Do not neglect to show hospitality to strangers, for by this some have entertained angels without knowing it" (Heb 13:1-2). The author of Hebrews is reminding us that Abraham showed hospitality to three complete strangers, who looked to Abraham like ordinary men passing through town. However, it was later revealed that they were more than men.

Let's look at the details and context of this story found in Genesis 18. Abram was born and raised a pagan idol-worshipper in Mesopotamia, 500 miles east of Canaan, for the first seventy-five years of his life (Gen 12:4; Josh 24:2). While a complete stranger and foreigner to YHWH, God called and saved Abram and blessed him in many ways. God promised to bless Abram by making him a great nation and giving his descendants the Promised Land (in Canaan, Num 13:2). also blessing all the nations of the world through Abram by bringing the Messiah through his lineage. God ratified these promises by changing Abram's name to Abraham, by making an unconditional covenant with Abraham (Gen 15), and by ratifying the covenant with a sign—circumcision (Gen 17). To begin the fulfillment of these promises, Abraham's wife Sarah needed to have a son, but she was barren her whole life (Gen 16:1). Abraham waited for twenty-four years until God finally took initiative by allowing Sarah, a barren old woman, to become pregnant...at the age of ninety! God purposed to announce this amazing news to Abraham one year in advance by coming down from heaven and making a personal visit to Abraham, who was now ninety-nine years old. This is where Genesis 18 begins and the great scene of Abraham's hospitality is described as follows:

Now the LORD appeared to him by the oaks
of Mamre, while he was sitting at the tent
door in the heat of the day. When he lifted
up his eyes and looked, behold, three men
were standing opposite him; and when he
saw them, he ran from the tent door to meet
them and bowed himself to the earth, and
said, "My Lord, if now I have found favor in
Your sight, please do not pass Your servant
by. Please let a little water be brought and
wash your feet, and rest yourselves under the
tree; and I will bring a piece of bread, that
you may refresh yourselves; after that you
may go on, since you have visited your
servant." And they said, "So do, as you have
said." So Abraham hurried into the tent to
Sarah, and said, "Quickly, prepare three
measures of fine flour, knead it and make
bread cakes." Abraham also ran to the herd,
and took a tender and choice calf and gave it
to the servant, and he hurried to prepare it.
He took curds and milk and the calf which
he had prepared, and placed it before them;
and he was standing by them under the tree
as they ate.

Before highlighting the details of the hospitality scene,
a few big picture observations are in order regarding
chapter 18. First, verses one through eight serve as a

prelude to the main point of the chapter, which is that YHWH has come to Abraham in physical form to announce the good news that his eighty-nine year old barren wife, Sarah, will give birth to the promised seed in one year's time, at the age of ninety! Second, Abraham's hospitable, welcoming, generous spirit toward three complete strangers in this chapter is in complete contrast to the way the citizens of Sodom treated the same strangers as depicted in Genesis 19. The Bible shows through contrast that the moral state of people is often indicated by their treatment of strangers. As such, Abraham's character proves stellar. Third, at this point in his life at age ninety-nine, God had made Abraham "very rich" (13:2). He owned flocks and herds, silver and gold, servants and maids, camels and donkeys (24:35). He had his own militia who served under his command (14:14-15). He was highly respected and feared by regional leaders and kings (12:20; 14:17). In light of Abraham's elevated status and high stature, his lowly servant's attitude and actions toward the unknown strangers in Genesis 18 become even more impressive.

At the time, Abraham was living as a nomad in Hebron, eighteen miles south of Jerusalem and twenty-five miles west of the Dead Sea. He was sitting at the door of his tent in "the heat of the day" (the time of the main meal), when he looked up and saw "three men" standing right in front of him. He did not see them approaching—they just appeared as if out of nowhere, unnoticed. Instead of taking a defensive posture out of fear or paranoia from being caught off-guard by the three uninvited guests, Abraham's reaction was quite unexpected. He immediately ran up to them and bowed down to the earth, a universal sign of elaborate greeting, humility, welcome, and even deference. He did not call for his bodyguard or servants to protect him by screening the unknown visitors. He did not call for his personal militia of 400 warriors to frisk and vet the intruders. Unlike the Apostle Peter, he did not pull out his sword and start wailing away at their heads in desperation. Keep in mind, at this point Abraham has no idea who exactly the strangers are, and yet he will offer himself as their "servant" (v. 3).

Next, Abraham speaks to one of the three men and offers several gestures of practical kindness: he calls him "Lord" (Heb. *adonai*) out of respect; he pleads with the visitors to stay; he offers to wash their feet; he offers them shade from the hot sun under his terebinth trees; he offers bread for food and rest for their weary bodies. Even though Abraham is legitimately a "Master" and "Lord" over others, he assumes the role of servant here. The three strange men agreed to Abraham's invitation of welcome.

What happens next is also extraordinary. The text says Abraham "hurried" to follow through on all the promises he just made to his guests. We do not know what Abraham was doing just prior to their arrival as far as his agenda for the evening, whether it was a planned meal with his large household, or a date night with Sarah, or plotting out travel plans for the next day, or hammering out details of a peace treaty with a nearby village chieftain. It did not matter. Abraham put everything on hold on the spot in deference to his newly arrived guests. From his perspective, hands-on, personalized service and hospitality to them was paramount. He does not complain about being too busy or that their intrusion was inconvenient. He employs the heart of a servant and puts their needs before his own. And as we see from the text, he expects his wife Sarah, the queen of the home, to have the same spontaneous deferential spirit...despite her evening plans and lack of forewarning. And to Sarah's credit, she accommodates the unforeseen request.

Sarah was receptive as she quickly began to bake cakes for the visiting strangers while Abraham chose a calf to be slaughtered and cooked. When the fresh meat was cooked to perfection, Abraham acted like the waiter and took the meat, some curds and milk and presented it to the three guests, as they were waiting under the shady trees of Mamre. Out of courtesy for his guests, he stood by them the whole time while they ate their meal, ready to tend to their needs. All in all, Abraham's exemplary act of hospitality must have consumed just a few hours that day in view of all the preparations that he and Sarah provided. A few hours of selfless love toward some strangers became a model of godly hospitality for the ages.

Hebrews 13 commends Abraham for his gracious hospitality on this occasion. The Hebrews author also notes that Abraham did not know at first that the "three men" he chose to welcome were more than men—they were angels! Two of the angels were in the form of human men (Gen 19:1), and one of the angels was the LORD Himself in bodily form, a theophany—possibly the pre-incarnate Christ (18:1, 17)!

God calls Christians to be as hospitable as Abraham was to these three strangers. What are the practical takeaways to be aware of as we seek to love strangers after the pattern of the great patriarch? First, Abraham loved God and he was a friend of God (James 2:23). We cannot love others, especially strangers, in a real and deep way in our own strength. We can love only because God first loved us (1 John 4:19). God called Abram when he was seventy-five and saved him shortly thereafter (Gen 15:6). Abraham had the capacity to love strangers because God loved him and in return, he loved God. Christians have that same supernatural capacity. Scripture says that as a result of salvation, the love of God has been shed abroad in our hearts (Rom 5:5). There is no excuse for a believer to shun strangers or fail to love them.

Second, Abraham lived by faith (Heb 11:9). He trusted God for his needs. As he hurried to pick a calf for slaughter, he never gave a second thought as to what the meal would cost him or how much he would lose in the process. He did not stop to think if he would be reimbursed. He did not think to himself, "Boy, I hope they appreciate this!" or, "I sure hope I get something in return from these three guys." There were no conditions or inhibitions with his acts of kindness. He knew this world was not his home. He held on to this world's goods with a loose grip. If we want to be hospitable to real strangers then it is going to take faith on our part. We will need to trust God beyond our own thinking, limits, and comfort zone. But living by faith is not an option—it is an imperative for all believers (Hab 2:4; 2 Cor 5:7).

Third, Abraham was prepared. Because he was prepared, Abraham could act immediately. Many people are not in a position to entertain guests without warning…for many reasons. A husband may want to help someone on the fly, but he may find resistance from family members or his wife. Not so with Abraham. He and Sarah were on the same page in this regard. They had cultivated a relationship that welcomed such unforeseen hospitality. Sarah respected her husband (1 Pet 3:6). Their living quarters were also prepared to accommodate a few guests at a moment's notice. Sadly, many people can't say the same—the ill state of their living quarters prohibits helping others as the needs arise. They are not prepared to fulfill this biblical mandate.

Fourth, Abraham had a proper view of himself. He was willing to be a servant. Just because he was a wealthy sheikh, the head of the home, influential, the commander of an army, a patriarch, a prophet, and feared by nearby kings, he was not prevented from literally getting down on his knees in service to the needs of these three strangers. Remember, at this time Abraham was ninety-nine, a seasoned old man. But he does not use his age as an excuse to delegate all the work to his younger servants. That takes true humility and an awareness of one's true lowly status compared to God's greatness as Creator, Savior, and Judge. God has called us and commissioned us to love others through selfless service (John 13:14; Gal 5:13). Abraham obeyed and was blessed (Gen 24:1; 26:5).

Finally, Abraham's hospitality was thorough or comprehensive. He did not just offer a cup of water or a ten-minute respite for his visitors, or a Band-Aid on the fly. He provided a hearty, home-cooked full-course meal, extended rest in the shade out of the brutal midday sun, a foot washing, and hands-on service as their personal servant for the duration. It is this thorough, holistic, personalized approach to hospitality that makes Abraham's deed stand out in history as the exemplar to esteem and follow. It is also from this scenario that the idea of a meal or providing food would forever be attached conceptually as an inherent part of the definition of biblical hospitality. It is possible to be hospitable without an attendant meal or provision of food, but the Bible places major significance to the fellowship meal in hospitality contexts. The epitome of this idea is illustrated by Jesus several times in the

Gospels where He says many strangers will be invited to His fellowship meal in the future kingdom while the "sons of the kingdom" will be cast out (Matt 8:10-12; cf. 22:1-14).

Rebekah

Another classic Old Testament example of biblical stranger-love comes from the life of Rebekah, Abraham's daughter-in-law. At the end of Abraham's life, when he was around 140 years of age, he commissioned his most trusted servant to find a wife for his son Isaac (Gen 24:1-3). Isaac was close to forty years old. He did not want Isaac marrying a local Canaanite, so Abraham sent his servant 450 miles north to a town called Nahor in northwest Mesopotamia (modern Turkey). There, Abraham believed a wife from his own relatives could be found. Abraham believed God would providentially guide his servant in the whole process (24:7). The servant took off on the long, arduous journey accompanied by some attendants along with ten camels. Upon finally reaching his destination, the servant gave his camels a rest and had them kneel down near a well. It was evening time and they all needed water. Abraham's servant was a man of faith and so as a complete stranger, hundreds of miles from home, in need of food, water and lodging, the servant prayed and asked God for help and guidance.

As he was still praying God answered his prayer. A young woman approached the well with a jar on her shoulder and went down to the spring of water to fill her jar. At that moment, Abraham's servant ran up to her and said, "Please let me drink a little water from your jar" (v. 17). Keep in mind, Abraham's servant was an out-of-towner, unfamiliar, and a complete stranger to Rebekah. All this makes her response to him remarkable. Instead of shying away, startled, from the stranger's request from fear, uncertainty, or self-protection, she responded with this:

> [18] She said, "Drink, my lord"; and she quickly lowered her jar to her hand, and gave him a drink. [19] Now when she had finished giving him a drink, she said, "I will draw also for your camels until they have finished drinking." [20] So she quickly emptied her jar into the trough, and ran back to the well to draw, and she drew for all his camels. [21] Meanwhile, the man was gazing at her in silence, to know whether the LORD had made his journey successful or not (24:18-21).

Watering camels is hard work because they are large animals and they drink a lot. Rebekah fed ten of them on the spot. When the camels finished drinking, Rebekah then revealed who her family was and extended further hospitality blessings to the stranger as she told him, "We have both plenty of straw and feed, and room to lodge in" (v. 25). Spontaneously, she invited the stranger and his attendants to lodge at her home and she also promised to feed all of his camels.

Rebekah was an exemplary kind, courteous, and hospitable woman. Gracious hospitality probably ran in the family, for her brother Laban was equally hospitable when he met Abraham's servant for the first time. After hearing the initial report from Rebekah about the visiting entourage, Laban found Abraham's servant at the well and said, "Come in, blessed of the LORD! Why do you stand outside since I have prepared the house, and a place for the camels?" (v. 31). The servant complied, took him up on the offer and entered Laban's house, whereupon Laban, "unloaded the camels, and he gave straw and feed to the camels, and water to wash his feet and the feet of the men who were with him" (v. 32). The historical account closes telling how, in God's providence, Rebekah would return with Abraham's servant to Beersheba to marry Isaac. Rebekah then gave birth to Esau and Jacob, and Jacob would have twelve sons, forming the promised nation of Israel.

The hospitality extended by Rebekah and her brother Laban has many parallels to Abraham's hospitality to the three men. They lavished uninhibited concern, care, and comfort upon complete strangers. That is biblical hospitality.

The Old Testament Pattern

Many more examples of pious hospitality are illustrated in the Old Testament. Reuel the priest of Midian, also known as Jethro (Exod 3:1), welcomed Moses into his home for bread and lodging, when Moses was a complete stranger to him and a fugitive at that (2:20-21). The Canaanite woman Rahab, a citizen of Jericho who lived about 1400 BC, graciously invited two unknown Israelite spies into her home, providing protection and showing these strangers "kindness" (Josh 2:12). The two Israelite foreigners told her of YHWH and His greats works. Her heart was convicted, she became a believer (2:11), and God rewarded her for her kind hospitality shown toward these two aliens (Josh 6:17; Heb 11:3; Jam 2:25).

Fast forward 300 years to the days of Samson the judge. Samson's father was Manoah, a Danite living thirteen miles southwest of Jerusalem. The book of Judges describes how Manoah and his wife extended a courteous gesture of hospitality to a complete stranger saying, "Please let us detain you so that we may prepare a young goat for you" (13:15). King David (1,000-960 BC) was no stranger to hospitality. He was received as a stranger by many for years when he was fleeing from Saul and Absalom (1 Sam 21-22). He returned the grace by being hospitable to needy strangers like Chimham (2 Sam 19:38) and the lame man, Mephibosheth (2 Sam 9).

The virtuous woman of Proverbs 31 (possibly Solomon's mother, cf. 31:1) is known for many godly traits and attitudes. One that stands out is hospitality, for "She extends her hand to the poor, and she stretches out her hands to the needy." The godly woman is hospitable by way of attitude and habit. The fact that this woman "stretches out" means that she is deliberate, proactive and even aggressive at meeting the needs of those around her, specifically the "poor" and the "needy," which in Old Testament times was often "strangers" who were passing through.

The most unique form of stranger-love required by God in the Old Testament was the law regarding the cities of refuge. "It was also the duty of the elders of the cities of refuge to succor, as well as to protect, the unwitting killer who sought refuge in their cities until the death of the high priest (Num 35:9-34)."[2] There were six cities of refuge: Kedesh, Shechem, Hebron, Bezer, Ramoth and Golan (Josh 20:7-8). Many more examples could be put forth, but these sufficiently make the case for God's imperative of hospitality made plain in the Old Testament.

3

JESUS AND HOSPITALITY

The New Testament world of Jesus, the apostles, and the Church practiced a generic and universal form of hospitality—almost a compulsory and rudimentary expectation of helping sojourners, travelers, strangers and aliens as they came passing through one's town. This custom was a result of nomadic life that typified the Old Testament world, as the Near East had much desert and wilderness terrain. Bedouins were common and sedentary life was rare. Green pastures for animal life and sustenance were seasonal and migratory. Abraham was an alien on the move (Heb 11:8-9). Isaac was a traveler (Gen 26:1). Jacob was a sojourner (Gen 28-29). Jacob's sons were nomads (Gen 31:17-21). They were all practitioners and beneficiaries of stranger-love. As a result, God codified this common-grace practice of welcoming pilgrims and strangers into the Mosaic Law, hallowing it as a universal ethic. As such, welcoming strangers from abroad was the common practice and expectation of the Jews in Israel during the days of Jesus and the apostles. Ironically the Gospels reveal an inconsistency about hospitality with respect to Jesus. On the one hand, Jesus was frequently denied the hospitality He deserved, yet He Himself was the Master at practicing and preaching the ideals of hospitality. This chapter highlights that dissonance.

Born in a Manger

The first example of hospitality we meet in the Gospels is actually a negative one, and the greatest miscarriage or negligence of hospitality the world has ever known. That is how Jesus, the Savior of the World, was ignored and even rejected as a visiting stranger. This is true spiritually as well as practically. Spiritually speaking, the Gospel of John opens up immediately identifying Jesus as God in the flesh, who came to earth motivated by love to save sinners, beginning with the divine visit to His own people and nation, Israel. But instead of opening their hearts and homes to Him, they spurned Him. John recounts in hindsight, "He came to His own, and those who were His own did not receive Him" (1:11). This verse teaches that Jesus came down from heaven to be the Savior of Israel and the world, but particularly the Jewish leadership, did not welcome Him. They were not hospitable. John says Israel "did not receive" Him. The Greek word for "receive" is *paralambano*, the common New Testament word that can mean "to welcome." The essence of being hospitable is to have a welcoming spirit toward another. On the whole, Jesus was not welcomed when He came 2,000 years ago.

John says Jesus came to "His own," so there was a sense in which He was not a stranger. He was not a stranger in that He was a fellow Jew. Also, He was the One predicted in the Old Testament Jewish Scriptures, so they should have been expecting His arrival and should have been able to identify Him (Matt 2:1-6). And generically He should not have been a stranger for He was the Creator of all things—including them! (John 1:1, 3, 10).

But in a real sense Jesus was indeed a stranger to many. He was a stranger to Jerusalem Jews because He was raised for thirty years in Nazareth of Galilee. The Jerusalem Jewish leadership looked down their noses at those outside the Jerusalem enclave. Even after two-plus years of public ministry, the multitudes who followed Him and benefitted from His miracles were continually debating His identity. He was strange and foreign to them because they did not know who His earthly father was (John 6:42); they did not know where He was trained or why He taught so differently than other rabbis (Matt 7:28). Many asked Him, rudely, point-blank in public, while He was teaching, "Who are you?" (John 8:25; cf. John 4:29; 5:12; 9:36; 12:34; Matt 21:10; 26:63). Conspiracy theories about Him were flourishing among the Jews. At the end of His public ministry some Jews were speculating that He was John the Baptist risen from the dead. Others conjectured that He was Elijah the prophet or Jeremiah reincarnated. And still others promulgated the intriguing myth that He was a great Old Testament prophet risen from the dead (Matt 16:14; Luke 9:19). Worse still, the Jewish leadership labeled Him a bastard child (John 8:41), a genetically polluted Samaritan (John 8:48), demon-possessed (John 8:52), a false teacher (John 7:47-48) and a blasphemer worthy of death (Matt 26:65-66).

In addition to being rejected as a stranger on the spiritual level, Jesus and His family were rejected at the time of His birth. Ironically, YHWH, the God of the Jews, was the one who originally made the law for compulsory hospitality to be shown by Jews toward visitors who pass their way in time of need (Lev 19:10). But when the greatest Jew in the history of the world came visiting (in utero) to a fellow Jewish town with His poor family (Luke 2:24; cf. Lev 12:6-8), He along with His humble Jewish family were categorically not-welcomed by fellow Jews. They did not benefit from the law of hospitality that should have been their safety net.

The Gospel of Luke describes the historical context of Jesus' birth in Bethlehem:

> Now in those days a decree went out from Caesar Augustus, that a census be taken of all the inhabited earth. ² This was the first census taken while Quirinius was governor

of Syria. ³ And everyone was on his way to register for the census, each to his own city. ⁴ Joseph also went up from Galilee, from the city of Nazareth, to Judea, to the city of David which is called Bethlehem, because he was of the house and family of David, ⁵ in order to register along with Mary, who was engaged to him, and was with child. ⁶ While they were there, the days were completed for her to give birth. ⁷ And she gave birth to her firstborn son; and she wrapped Him in cloths, and laid Him in a manger, because there was no room for them in the inn (2:1-7).

As Jesus was about to be born of Mary, she was living in Nazareth of Galilee with Joseph, seventy miles north of Bethlehem. All of Israel at the time was under the domination of the Roman Empire and its emperor, Caesar Augustus (63 BC-AD 14). Augustus, the adopted son of Julius Caesar, had issued a mandate that all citizens enroll in a census in their home towns. Joseph was from Bethlehem, so he took his pregnant wife on the long, arduous journey to Bethlehem. While in Bethlehem, Jesus was born of Mary. At birth, baby Jesus was placed "in a manger." The Greek word for "manger," *phatne*, simply refers to an animal feeding trough. It does not necessarily mean Jesus was born in a stable. It is possible the manger was in a cave where animals were kept. The Bible is not specific on the matter. The Bible is clear, though, that Mary, Joseph, and Jesus were placed among a bunch of animals at the time the Savior was born. Luke says, "there was no room for them in the inn." The word for "inn" does not refer to a hotel. It is a generic term referring to a general lodging place or guest room, and in this case could have been nothing more than a makeshift shelter thrown together to accommodate the overwhelming influx of visitors from abroad who came to the town for the mandatory census. This means that no one in the city of Bethlehem took Mary and Joseph into their house as she was about to give birth while they were temporarily in town for the census. They were strangers, fellow Jews, passing through, in need of some caring love and accommodations. The Son of God was about to enter the world in fulfillment of countless Hebrew prophecies (i.e., Micah 5:2; Isa 7:14; 9:6). If anyone deserved unreserved welcoming hospitality, it was Jesus the Messiah and His family. But such was not the case.

Today in our culture we celebrate births and announce them from the rooftops...and on the Internet, for all to know. The God-Man was virtually ignored when He was born in obscurity. Such a beginning for Jesus' earthly life was only fitting for His life-long role as the Suffering Servant who would be acquainted with grief and rejection (Isa 53). One commentator states it poignantly:

No angels appeared, as they later would to
the shepherds. No heavenly trumpets rang.
No voice from heaven announced the birth
of the Son of God. Alone except for her
young husband, far from her family and
friends, in the most primitive conditions, a
young girl gave birth. Thus did the second
person of the Trinity step from eternity into
time and space….Mary was forced to give
birth in the only place available—the place
where the travelers' animals were kept. When
Jesus came into the world, He was born in
the most comfortless conditions—a smelly,
filthy, chilly, shelter, surrounded by noisy
animals. It was a fitting entrance for the "Son
of Man [who had] nowhere to lay His head"
(Luke 9:58).[1]

After Jesus' birth, the vassal pseudo-king of the Jews,
Herod the Great, tried to murder baby Jesus out of
jealousy and fear (Matt 2:3, 13). Warned by an angel,
Joseph fled to Egypt with his family as an enraged and
deranged Herod slaughtered all the male children two
years and under in Bethlehem and its surrounding
regions (2:16). Herod, the "king of the Jews," should
have welcomed the greatest King of the Jews, the
Messiah, with open arms, reverence and rejoicing. But
instead the visiting family of the Savior was literally run
out of the country for a time (Matt 2:19-21). In the end,

the only ones to welcome Jesus and His family at the time of His birth were nameless shepherds from the fields (Luke 2:8), a Jewish prophet named Simeon (Luke 2:25), Anna, the aged prophetess (2:36), and strange Gentile sojourners from the east, known as the magi (Matt 2:1-2).

The Suffering Servant

Fast forward thirty years and the Scriptures reveal that Jesus fared no better in receiving hospitality from others. For the most part He was neglected, ignored, or deprived when it came to material possessions and practical comforts. He noted this plight when He declared publicly about Himself, "The foxes have holes and the birds of the air have nests, but the Son of Man has nowhere to lay His head" (Matt 8:20). Once Jesus left the home of Mary and began His public ministry, He was homeless. Jesus was a homeless person—that is what this verse means, and that is a provocative reality. For three-plus years Jesus had an itinerant ministry. He was always traveling and on the move. He would have benefitted from Old Testament hospitality from fellow Israelites. He restricted His ministry to the Jews and their cities and towns, as He preached the good news, taught the masses, healed the sick and loved sinners. All the while, He never had a home to call His own. He depended on the Father to provide for Him (Matt 6:8) and at times a few hospitable Israelites actually welcomed Him into their homes as a stranger in need

(Luke 8:1-3). But much of the time Jesus had no place to live. Ironically, Jesus promised to build grand, heavenly mansions for His followers (John 14:2-3) while at the same time He had no earthly home of His own. Even more ironic is the fact that Jesus is the Creator (John 1:3) and sovereign one who actually owns everything on earth (1 Cor 10:26), alongside the Father (John 17:5), and yet during His ministry He had nothing. One Bible teacher aptly describes the implications of Jesus' homelessness:

> In His humiliation He did not even have the basic comforts of life. Jesus had no place of His own—no house or property, not even a tent. After the dispute about Jesus' healing of the blind man, "everyone went to his home," John tells us: "But Jesus went to the Mount of Olives" (John 7:53-8:1). Whereas others went home to spend the night, Jesus spent it alone under the stars, in prayer with His Father. We are told of His often spending time in the home of Peter in Capernaum and of Mary, Martha, and Lazarus in Bethany, but we are never told of His spending even an hour in His own house, because He had none.[2]

It was noted earlier that John said Jesus came to His own, and His own received Him not. This lack of a welcoming spirit existed even among Jesus' blood relatives. Jesus had several siblings or half-brothers and half-sisters, for Mary gave birth to several children after Jesus. Jesus was Mary's first-born (Luke 2:78). Jesus' younger siblings were the brothers, James, Joseph, Jude, Simon and some sisters (Matt 13:55-56). Jesus left home and began public ministry when He was thirty (Luke 3:23). After Jesus began His ministry, demanding that all follow Him, His own siblings refused to welcome Him. They were anything but hospitable. At one point, His brothers overtly questioned His motives, and mocked Him, and taunted Him (John 7:3-5). The lack of hospitality shown to Jesus during His life and ministry 2,000 years ago was broad and deep. Fortunately, God's grace would change the hearts of His brothers, James and Jude, and they would follow Jesus as the Savior after His resurrection (1 Cor 15:7; Jude 1).

Contrary to the lack of hospitality Jesus was shown, He Himself was the master and model of showing hospitality to others. From the biblical definition and pattern already established, it is clear that at the heart of hospitality is the love of strangers, which entails loving people in general, greeting unfamiliar ones with arms wide open, attending to the practical needs of others, and aggressively meeting those needs selflessly and sacrificially if necessary...like a sincere, warm greeting of shalom, foot-washing, providing a meal or a bed for rest and more. Jesus was characterized by all of these attributes.

Jesus exuded a true love for people in general, and strangers in particular. Jesus had no rivals in this regard. He was incarnate love. Jesus truly welcomed sinners. Not only did He welcome them, He pursued them! His whole ministry was given to loving, welcoming, serving, and caring for strangers—people He did not know. Jesus loved the multitudes (Matt 9:36), as He wept for them (Matt 23:37) and prayed for them (Luke 23:34) and even gave His life for them (John 3:16).

Jesus' truly welcoming spirit is seen in His willingness to touch a leper. Lepers were outcasts and despised by the people. The one thing you should never do is go near a leper, let alone touch one. On one occasion, while ministering by the Sea of Galilee, Jesus did the unthinkable and touched a man full of leprosy (Luke 5:13). The man was instantly healed. On another occasion as He was passing through Samaria, Jesus came across ten leprous men who were complete strangers (Luke 17:11 ff.). They may have been part of an isolated leper colony—literally strangers to everyone in town. When they heard Jesus was close by, traveling through their village, they cried out, "Have mercy on us!" Jesus did and He healed them. Jesus loved strangers. Even unclean, ostracized, defiled, dirty, deplorable, outcast strangers like lepers. True hospitality—the act of welcoming those in need, especially strangers—flows from a heart of love and compassion for people. Jesus was the Master.

Another unparalleled act of welcoming hospitality on the part of Jesus was when He was invited to Simon the Pharisee's house for a meal (Luke 7:36-50). This may be the only time a Pharisee invited Jesus into his home. Simon seemed to have an open home and was a practitioner of the common grace of hospitality rooted in the Old Testament ethic. For that, Simon was to be commended. As such, Jesus was not the only guest in Simon's home that day. As Jesus and Simon were reclining on the floor for the meal, suddenly a woman appeared behind them with a jar of precious perfume. She was weeping and began wetting Jesus' feet with her tears, anointing His feet with the perfume and wiping His feet with her hair. By her appearance it was obvious she was a "sinner" from the city, probably an immoral woman. When Simon saw her he was startled, disgusted, and perturbed that Jesus let her touch His feet.

Jesus knew Simon's judgmental, unloving, unwelcoming thoughts and began to expose his inhospitable heart with a short parable and a direct rebuke. Luke recounts the details of the exchange:

[44] Turning toward the woman, He said to Simon, "Do you see this woman? I entered your house; you gave Me no water for My feet, but she has wet My feet with her tears and wiped them with her hair. [45] You gave Me no kiss; but she, since the time I came in, has not ceased to kiss My feet. [46] You did not

anoint My head with oil, but she anointed My feet with perfume. [47] For this reason I say to you, her sins, which are many, have been forgiven, for she loved much; but he who is forgiven little, loves little." [48] Then He said to her, "Your sins have been forgiven." [49] Those who were reclining *at the table* with Him began to say to themselves, "Who is this *man* who even forgives sins?" [50] And He said to the woman, "Your faith has saved you; go in peace."

In this stunning exchange, Jesus rebukes Simon the Pharisee for his lack of hospitality in three ways. At the same time Jesus commends the strange, unnamed sinful woman for being a paragon of virtue in showing hospitality towards the Savior in a home that was not even hers. First, Jesus embarrasses Simon, the host, by pointing out that he did not offer to wash Jesus' feet as Jesus entered his home as the special guest—a common practice and basic protocol in the day. Foot washing was expected, basic hospitality in biblical times (Gen 18:4; 19:2; 24:32; 43:24; Judges 19:21; John 12:3; 13:5; 1 Tim 5:10). This was a clear sign that Simon was not welcoming to Jesus. Jesus then points out that the woman lavishly and reverently washed Jesus' feet...not with lukewarm water and a rag, but with her fresh tears of devotion and her hair! Second, Simon did not greet Jesus with the kiss of peace, another common, expected sign of warm, welcoming hospitality (Gen 29:13; Acts 20:37; Rom 16:16; 1 Cor 16:20). It's as though Simon did not care about Jesus at all but instead had a hidden agenda. The sinful woman, on the other hand, kissed Jesus' feet nonstop from the time she entered the house—an act of sincere devotion and even worship. Third, Jesus put in stark relief Simon's lack of hospitality by noting that Simon did not anoint Jesus whereas the woman anointed Jesus' feet with valuable perfume.

This woman was a complete stranger and yet she gave Jesus the most personalized, loving, deliberate, uninhibited loving acts of hospitality imaginable. Her actions revealed her heart—she had a heart overflowing with love toward Christ. Simon's actions revealed his heart—he had a self-serving agenda and a judgmental attitude, and was void of all hospitality as a result.

Teaching on Hospitality

In addition to Jesus' acts of hospitality toward others, there is His teaching on hospitality. The story, or parable, of the Good Samaritan is the quintessential example. This parable may be one of the most well-known, time-tested, universally recognized stories ever told. Countless buildings, hospitals, churches, groups, organizations (secular and religious), masterful works of art, pieces of literature and para-church ministries have been named after it and inspired by it for 2,000 years. Being a "Good Samaritan" is a standard catchword to describe one who is a model of virtue. Amazingly, this parable that Jesus originated is only six verses long in the Bible. Jesus spoke the parable in response to a self-righteous Jewish scribe:

> But wishing to justify himself, he said to Jesus, "And who is my neighbor?" Jesus replied and said, "A man was going down from Jerusalem to Jericho, and fell among robbers, and they stripped him and beat him, and went away leaving him half dead. And by chance a priest was going down on that road, and when he saw him, he passed by on the other side. Likewise a Levite also, when he came to the place and saw him, passed by on the other side. But a Samaritan, who was on a journey, came upon him; and when he saw him, he felt compassion, and came to him and bandaged up his wounds, pouring oil and wine on *them*; and he put him on his own beast, and brought him to an inn and took care of him. On the next day he took out two denarii and gave them to the innkeeper and said, 'Take care of him; and whatever more you spend, when I return I will repay you.' Which of these three do you think proved to be a neighbor to the man who fell into the robbers' *hands*?" And he said, "The one who showed mercy toward him." Then Jesus said to him, "Go and do the same."

The first Great Commandment in the Bible is to love God (Deut 6:5) and the second, which flows from it and enables it, is to love your neighbor (Rom 13:9). Biblical hospitality is loving your neighbor who has a pressing practical need by sacrificially meeting that need, even if that neighbor is a stranger. All these key ingredients are present in the passage above. Jesus begins by affirming that everything begins with a true, complete love of God (vv. 28-29). Then, if you love God you have the capacity and obligation to love your neighbor. Jesus takes the mandate to love even further by showing that loving your neighbor is not limited to those you know or those you like. Loving your neighbor also means loving people you don't know and maybe even strangers you are not inclined to like. This is revolutionary and defies human logic, human tradition, human religion, and human preferences. It is a divine, supernatural capacity to love.

The lasting power in the Good Samaritan story centers around the Samaritan's attitude toward the injured stranger he saw laying half-dead on the road. When the Samaritan saw him the Bible says he "felt compassion" (v. 33) toward the helpless, injured man. "Compassion" here is the verbal form of the Greek word *splanchna*, a noun that literally refers to the intestines or the bowels or the inner parts of the stomach. It came to represent that pain in the gut which resulted from strong emotional turmoil during trials of life. It is similar to our modern-day expression, "heartbroken." The Samaritan had a true emotional, heart-felt sympathy of anguish for the bleeding stranger—and this sympathy prompted mercy and action. The injured man was Jewish, coming down from Jerusalem. The Samaritan was a half-breed, a half-Jew, an impure Jew, with a polluted mongrel ethnicity. Traditionally, full-blooded Judean Jews despised Samaritans, and the respectable Jew would have no dealings with them whatsoever, as Samaritans were considered "unclean." (John 4:9).

The Samaritan's heart-felt compassion and act of mercy is in stark contrast to the Jewish priest and the Jewish Levite who passed by their fellow dying Jew, as they looked at him with indifference—a cold heart and zero compassion. The priest and the Levite were clerics—men of the cloth, men who were supposed to represent God and serve the people. Not only that, the injured man was a Jewish pilgrim, and it was the Jewish pilgrims who gave alms at the Temple that provided for the sustenance of the priests and the Levites who were supposed to be serving and representing the lay Jewish people, like this man who lay dying in need of their help. Jesus' point is obvious: the priest and Levite performed religion, but they did not truly love God from the heart, and as a result they had no love for their fellow man. The Samaritan was different. His heart was different, therefore his attitude and actions were different. He showed the dying stranger the fullness of mercy and hospitality, or stranger-love, as he did not "pass by" but came up to him, poured oil on his injuries, bandaged his wounds, put him on his animal and transported him to an inn to receive care. The Samaritan then paid all the lodging fees accrued at the inn. The Samaritan's schedule was no doubt interrupted and changed by this whole event and he spent much of his own money to care for this man. Jesus commended this kind of overflowing generous, spontaneous hospitality and called on all His listeners that day to "Go and do the same" (vs. 37).

Another important teaching on hospitality by Jesus is from His Olivet Discourse that He gave at the end of His ministry in Matthew 25. Here Jesus taught that we are going to someday be judged, and one component of that judgment is going to be hospitality. How did we as believers and the Church practice or not practice hospitality? Jesus is going to use that in judgment towards us, whether it's through rewards or removal of rewards.

Matthew 25:31-40 is a very well-known passage that is often quoted out of context, so it can be confusing. In this passage there are applications specifically regarding hospitality and how we treat strangers. The context is about Judgment Day, and it is important to look closely at what Jesus says. He's judging the goats and the sheep, or believers and unbelievers. Verses 31-40 read,

But when the Son of Man comes in His glory, and all the angels with Him, then He will sit on His glorious throne. All the nations will be gathered before Him; and He will separate them from one another, as the shepherd separates the sheep from the goats; and He will put the sheep on His right, and the goats on the left. Then the King will say to those on His right, "Come, you who are blessed of My Father, inherit the kingdom prepared for you from the foundation of the world. For I was hungry, and you gave Me something to eat; I was thirsty, and you gave Me something to drink; **I was a stranger, and you invited Me in**; naked, and you clothed Me; I was sick, and you visited Me; I was in prison, and you came to Me." Then the righteous will answer Him, "Lord, when did we see You hungry, and feed You, or thirsty, and give You something to drink? And when did we see You a stranger, and invite You in, or naked, and clothe You? When did we see You sick, or in prison, and come to You?" The King will answer and say to them, "Truly I say to you, to the extent that you did it to one of these brothers of Mine, even the least of them, you did it to Me."

The priority of hospitality is highlighted by Jesus here in verse 35. Illustrated here is a welcoming, accommodating, blessing, serving, loving spirit towards strangers and those who are in need. Biblical hospitality is extending the love of Christ to strangers, all who bear the image of God. And it is a universal expectation because Jesus addresses this warning to "all the nations" in verse 32. We were once strangers who have been welcomed into Christ's family. We should be motivated to welcome strangers in turn. We will be judged by Jesus regarding our hospitality and how we treat others.

The hospitality modeled and taught by Jesus 2,000 years ago has ongoing practical benefits for us today because Jesus still continues His ministry of hospitality toward sinners like me and you. Jesus is still loving strangers today. That is the truth of Ephesians 2. According to this passage, Jesus showed us (those who are now Christians) hospitality in a spiritual way. Most of the people in my church and network are not Jewish. I myself am a Gentile. I wasn't a part of the Old Testament community by lineage, and I wasn't part of the special people of God like Israel was since God's covenant with Abraham. Yet, Jesus Christ loved me and welcomed me as a stranger, spiritually speaking, even though I was not Jewish. That is Paul's point in Ephesians 2:11-13 which reads as follows:

> Therefore remember that formerly you, the Gentiles in the flesh, who are called

"Uncircumcision" by the so-called "Circumcision," which is performed in the flesh by human hands—remember that **you were** at that time separate from Christ, excluded from the commonwealth of Israel, and **strangers** to the covenants of promise, having no hope and without God in the world. But now in Christ Jesus you who formerly were far off have been brought near by the blood of Christ.

Not only does Jesus loves sinners, but according to verse twelve above He loves strangers.
He goes on in verses 14-16:

> For He Himself is our peace, who made both groups into one and broke down the barrier of the dividing wall, by abolishing in His flesh the enmity, which is the Law of commandments contained in ordinances, so that in Himself He might make the two into one new man, thus establishing peace, and might reconcile them both in one body to God through the cross, by it having put to death the enmity.

We are blessed recipients of God's reconciliation, even though we were strangers. That's the grace of God and the gospel of Jesus Christ, which is the very model of how we should practice hospitality. A parallel truth to the reality that God and Jesus reach out to strangers with love is Jesus' parable in Luke 14:16-24, which teaches the same truth highlighted by Paul in Ephesians 2.

4

HOSPITALITY IN THE BALANCE

More Blessed to Give

Just like every other command from God in Scripture, commands to be hospitable have a context, parameters, and balance. There are some scriptural exceptions, or cautions, to the rule. The Bible delineates those exceptions clearly so there is no ambiguity. In this chapter we will survey those exceptions in light of their context and parameters to ensure balance in this area.

Practicing hospitality is actually a blessing. After all, Jesus said, "It is more blessed to give than receive" (Acts 20:35), and being hospitable toward strangers in need is a real act of giving. My wife and I have come to realize this truth after serving in ministry together as a married couple the past three decades.

Early on in our marriage, right after I graduated from seminary, I worked at a church in children's ministry part-time while I taught the Bible full-time at a large Christian school in Los Angeles. I had six classes per day with thirty-five kids in each class, consisting of both seventh graders and seniors. That's 210 teenagers every day! It was exciting, exhausting, challenging and memorable. One year in particular, I remember having a quiet and withdrawn female student in my senior Bible class who did not speak much but had an interest in learning the Bible. She seemed to be somewhat of a loner as she was not hanging with the athletes or the academic geeks or the popular crowd. She was soft-spoken and courteous. I developed a bit of a rapport with her as "Mr. McManis," the Bible teacher. I was able to get her to talk more than she normally did with others.

As the last day of the school year was approaching I found out unintentionally that she did not have a dad and she was not getting along with her mom. Her mom actually despised her because this student was a Christian. She was eighteen. It turns out that her mom had just kicked her out of the house and would not let her come back home. As a result, she had no place to stay. That day when I got home I shared the news with my wife and asked her, "Can we house this girl for a while? She has nowhere to go." My wife did not know this girl from Adam…or Eve…but said, "Absolutely!" We took her into our tiny, cramped apartment the next day. She happily slept on the floor in the living room for two weeks until she found a long-term solution. She was very thankful and appreciated immensely the care my wife gave her during that time: home-cooked meals, someone to talk to and get advice from. She said she was truly blessed.

Lesson Learned

In hindsight, my wife and I have fond memories of that incident. We saw a need, took a step of faith—well aware of the Bible's teaching on hospitality and on how to treat those in need—and welcomed the girl in. Thirty years later we see that God would use that occasion to establish a pattern and an ongoing ministry that my wife and I have practiced ever since. After the student left we took in an autistic Christian man for three months to help him get back on his feet…in that same cramped, one-bedroom apartment. Thirty years later, he is living a fully independent life in another state, faithfully involved in a good local church.

We also had a Christian man stay in our home on occasion (the same small apartment). We would periodically see him on the highways of California, sitting on the side of the road, reading a Bible, with a hefty back pack and a sign that said, "Jesus Saves." He called himself a missionary to the highways of America, had a powerful testimony, and was committed to a local church. He had shared the gospel with at least one person in all forty-eight continental states. He called himself "Brother Lee" and he never asked or begged from us the whole time we knew him. We initiated contact with him simply by asking, "Do you need a ride?" Then a ten-year friendship ensued, and he told us of the ongoing work he was doing to help a fledgling church in Mexico.

The above three scenarios all happened before we had kids. Once the children started coming, (we have four), the hospitality continued. When we finally began renting a house that had a few rooms, we began opening up our home to people in need of a more long-term basis. For instance, we housed a teenage girl we knew from a previous church in Texas that we had served in before moving to California. She was a neighbor who had a troubled and broken home. We befriended her, brought her to church and youth group, told her the gospel and loved her. Shortly after we moved to California, she called us out of desperation as her life and family were falling apart. We flew her out to our home and took her in for several months. We had four children at this time. They had great attitudes as well and welcomed her into their home, treating her like a big sister.

Not long after she moved out, we took in a high school senior from our church when his dad got a job in another state and the teen needed to finish high school. He stayed with us for six weeks. On another occasion, a young nineteen-year-old man with no family had been visiting our church for several months. He needed some stability in his life. So again, I came home and asked my wife, "Can this young man stay with us?"

She said, "Well, I don't know him, but if you think we should, then let's do it." He moved in the next week. Eventually he secured a full-time job, became self-sufficient and moved out on his own.

When that young man moved out, we took in a college student from Indonesia who needed a place to stay. A friend from church asked us if we could accommodate her. We did not know her—she was a stranger. But, she had recently started attending our church. We interviewed her, then my wife and I prayed and talked it over, and welcomed her in. She lived with us almost two years. She helped take care of the kids in return for living with us. She became part of the family in a way. She finished school, graduated, moved out, married a Christian man and now has her own family. It was a blessed experience for all of us. Our four kids have fond memories of her.

A few years later, a single, divorced man with three teenagers and serious health and financial challenges began attending our church. I finally was able to sit down with him and hear his testimony. It was clear he was a believer who had been through many trying situations and was now at rock-bottom in life. He was living in his car. So once again I found myself going home to my wife, explaining this guy's situation, and asking her, "Can this man live with us until he can get his life together?" And once again, my wife, who did not know this man from Adam, said, "If you think we should, then invite him over." So we did. He lived with us for a while, complied by the house rules, was respectful of the family, never asked for anything, and eventually moved out on his own. I could recount at least five others we took into our home over the years, all with different needs and hurdles to overcome, who found refuge, solace, and stability by living with us which helped them transition into independence.

I personally give much credit to my wife and my four kids who maintained tremendously hospitable attitudes toward all these strangers over the years. They always seemed to have a stranger living in their house, eating their Cheerios, using their washing machine, sneaking in their back garage door into the downstairs bedroom. They often wondered, "That person finally moved out...that room is now vacant! Now who is dad going to bring home from work to live with us?" My four children, who are all about college age now, literally don't know what it is like to not have a stranger, or non-family member, living in their house.

In addition to the many random people from churches, and off the street, that we invited into our home, there are the countless visiting pastors, missionaries, and church guests from all over the world we were able to entertain when they needed a place to lodge—thirty years of fond memories, spending quality time with dear saints, many of whom were complete strangers. We thank God for the mandate and ministry of biblical hospitality. Jesus is right—it is more blessed to give than to receive.

Seven Cautions

Now I want to transition to the caution—hospitality does entail discretion, wisdom, and prayer. You can't take every person into your home who claims to have a need. This imperative can't be approached willy-nilly out of guilt, compulsion, lack of planning or ignorance. The Bible is clear about that. God wants us to be hospitable, but He also wants us to be good stewards. He wants to protect us. In light of those truths, consider seven kinds of people that Scripture says to avoid and keep your distance from—which also means you don't extend biblical hospitality to them.

False Teachers

The first group of people to avoid and stay aloof from is false teachers. These are people who profess to love God, say they help people, frequently quote the Bible and invoke the name of Jesus, but in fact are phonies. The Bible calls them spiritual imposters and says they are dangerous. They don't deserve any hospitality from true Christians. John the Apostle puts it this way in his second epistle:

> For many deceivers have gone out into the world, those who do not acknowledge Jesus Christ *as* coming in the flesh. This is the deceiver and the antichrist. Watch yourselves, that you do not lose what we have accomplished, but that you may receive a full reward. Anyone who goes too far and

does not abide in the teaching of Christ, does not have God; the one who abides in the teaching, he has both the Father and the Son. If anyone comes to you and does not bring this teaching, **do not receive him into *your* house**, and do not give him a greeting; for the one who gives him a greeting participates in his evil deeds.

The Bible says categorically in verse ten "do not receive him into your house." This literally means, "Do not be hospitable to false teachers! Do not welcome them." To some this sounds mean or not nice. But God knows this is actually a loving thing to do as it protects others from the poison of destructive spirituality and from deceivers with ill motives.

Immoral Professing Christians

The next group to stay away from is immoral people who claim to be Christians. We all have sin living in us and we all sin (Rom 7:14-24; 1 John 1:1, 10), but there is a different category of people who say they are believers while at the same time they nurture, protect and justify their sin. Sometimes they even flaunt their sin and have no regard for the holiness of God or the purity of the Church. Avoid such people. More than that, call them out and expose them. The apostle Paul put it this way in 1 Corinthians 5:

> I wrote you in my letter not to associate with immoral people; I *did* not at all *mean* with the immoral people of this world, or with the covetous and swindlers, or with idolaters, for then you would have to go out of the world. But actually, I wrote to you not to associate with any so-called brother if he is an immoral person, or covetous, or an idolater, or a reviler, or a drunkard, or a swindler—**not even to eat with such a one**.

The Bible says categorically, "not even to eat with such a one." This means, do not entertain them, do not be hospitable, do not welcome them; rather, isolate them. This is holy separation and blessed subtraction. To embrace and welcome such an immoral person would be to endorse that person and their wicked lifestyle that is contrary to being a disciple of Jesus. True believers don't willfully embrace and flaunt immoral living as a lifestyle. John says, "No one born of God makes a practice of sinning, for God's seed abides in him" (1 John 3:9).

Those in Church Discipline

The third group of people God's Word says not to welcome with hospitality is those under church discipline who are in step three or four—those living under corporate, public censure. Typically, such a person is a professing Christian, has refused numerous times to repent of sin and has been exposed by the local church. While they are unrepentant in steps three or four, other believers should not be welcoming them into fellowship nor should they be hospitable. Rather, the saints should be warning those remaining in sin and calling them to repentance. And if the person under discipline runs from the accountability of their home church to another church without repenting to hide from their sin, the new church should not welcome the recalcitrant spiritual fugitive. The new church needs to honor the discipline process of the home church in question. In such an instance, the new church is not to be a city of refuge for the rebel.

Sluggards

The fourth category of people the Bible says to not welcome with hospitable care is the sluggard. Paul calls such a person "the idle brother." This person is the able-bodied person who loiters around churches, lingering among the saints for the sole purpose of begging from others, feigning hardships, loaded with illegitimate excuses as to why they can't work. The Bible says to love and help the poor (Gal 2:10), but these "idle" people are the fake poor; lazy manipulators; bold, expectant sloths; presumptuous takers who prey on the good-hearted, kind and sympathetic givers. Scripture says not to aid and abet their self-centered behavior:

> Now we command you, brethren, in the
> name of our Lord Jesus Christ, that you keep
> away from every brother who leads an unruly

life and not according to the tradition which you received from us. For you yourselves know how you ought to follow our example, because we did not act in an undisciplined manner among you, nor did we eat anyone's bread without paying for it, but with labor and hardship we *kept* working night and day so that we would not be a burden to any of you; not because we do not have the right *to this*, but in order to offer ourselves as a model for you, so that you would follow our example. For even when we were with you, we used to give you this order: if anyone is not willing to work, then he is not to eat, either. For we hear that some among you are leading an undisciplined life, doing no work at all, but acting like busybodies. Now such persons we command and exhort in the Lord Jesus Christ to work in quiet fashion and eat their own bread.

This is tough love. Verse six says, "keep away from" them. Verse ten says, "If they don't work—then they don't eat."

Factious People
The fifth group of people Scripture commands us to avoid, thus depriving them of hospitality, are factious people. Titus 3:10 commands us to "reject a factious man." A factious person is one who is divisive,

argumentative, contentious, and known for causing cliques, factions, and schisms in the church—even after a couple resounding warnings from church leaders. Paul says further that such a person in the church is actually "foolish," (3:9) even "perverted and is sinning, being self-condemned" (3:11). Proverbs says, "Leave the presence of a fool" (14:7) and "Do not associate with a...hot-tempered man" (22:24).

Mockers

The sixth group of people the Bible says to avoid are mockers, or those who overtly scorn the gospel. Jesus was incarnate love, but at the same time He was not welcoming to everyone. There were people He avoided and hid from. These were people that He warned His own disciples to stay away from. The main people Jesus avoided were the Jewish leaders in Jerusalem. Many times He traveled in secret at feast time (John 7:10) for He knew they were trying to kill Him (7:19). These same Jewish leaders mocked Jesus publicly, calling Him a Samaritan, demonic, and a blasphemer. In return, He rejected them, saying, "where I am you cannot come" (John 8:34). Jesus told His disciples that if people reject their message then they were to shake the dust off of their feet and avoid them (Matt 10:14). He also told His followers to not cast their pearls before swine (Matt 7:6). Those who mock the gospel are to be shunned. Jesus further taught that if mockers die in their sin, refusing to repent, then Jesus will not welcome them into heaven:

> Not everyone who says to Me, "Lord, Lord," will enter the kingdom of heaven, but he who does the will of My Father who is in heaven *will enter.* Many will say to Me on that day, 'Lord, Lord, did we not prophesy in Your name, and in Your name cast out demons, and in Your name perform many miracles?' And then I will declare to them, 'I never knew you; DEPART FROM ME, YOU WHO PRACTICE LAWLESSNESS'" (Matt 7:21-23).

Dangerous People

The seventh group of people the Scripture says to watch out for and not welcome are dangerous people. In the Old Testament, God gave six cities of refuge that people could flee to in the event that they accidentally committed manslaughter (Num 35). A trial was held to verify that person's guilt or innocence. If the person was not guilty then that stranger to the city was to be embraced and welcomed. If the fugitive was guilty of willful murder then that person was not welcomed to the city and instead was summarily executed (35:16-21). God has always warned His people about those who are dangerous. God gave law and government to protect the innocent from those who threaten our well-being

and even our lives. This is not just an Old Testament
truth. First Timothy 1 says,

> [the] law is not made for a righteous person,
> but for those who are lawless and rebellious,
> for the ungodly and sinners, for the unholy
> and profane, for those who kill their fathers
> or mothers, for murderers and immoral men
> and homosexuals and kidnappers and liars
> and perjurers, and whatever else is contrary
> to sound teaching (vv. 9-10).

Paul says in Romans 13 that God has given laws of
government for the purpose of protecting innocent
citizens from dangerous people. Authorities like the
police and military are even given the power ("the
sword," 13:4) by God to execute capital punishment for
capital offenses:

> Every person is to be in subjection to the
> governing authorities. For there is no
> authority except from God, and those which
> exist are established by God. Therefore
> whoever resists authority has opposed the
> ordinance of God; and they who have
> opposed will receive condemnation upon
> themselves. For rulers are not a cause of fear
> for good behavior, but for evil. Do you want
> to have no fear of authority? Do what is
> good and you will have praise from the same;

for it is a minister of God to you for good. But if you do what is evil, be afraid; for it does not bear the sword for nothing; for it is a minister of God, an avenger who brings wrath on the one who practices evil.

The Bible is not naïve, and Christians should not be naïve either. This world is full of dangerous people and violent law-breakers. Such dangerous people should not be harbored, welcomed, protected or given sanctuary with disregard to just laws. God is the Great Law-giver and His laws need to be honored. Christians and the Church universal need to remember that the law is holy, just, and good (Rom 7:12). It should not be trumped or ignored in the name of misguided, undeserved mercy.

Giving is more blessed than receiving. Extending biblical hospitality in the name of Christ is a vital ministry and virtuous discipline. Yet it needs to be practiced with God's wisdom, leading and discretion to preserve safety for all and produce good stewardship. Thankfully, God's Word is the perfect, sufficient guide to help us strike the balance.

5

LIVING OUT THE MINISTRY OF HOSPITALITY

In this chapter let's consider some practical principles for implementing hospitality in our personal lives and in the local church.

It Begins With the Heart

True hospitality begins with the right heart and the right attitude. We've seen that hospitality means "stranger love." If we don't have a true love for people, then we will not be hospitable. If you are a Christian, then you have no excuse here. The Bible says that the love of God has been shed abroad in the heart of every true believer: "the love of God has been poured out within our hearts through the Holy Spirit who was given to us" (Rom 5:5). Remember, that "the love of God" is a unique kind of love—a love that unbelievers don't possess or have access to. It is a divine love enabling you to be selfless, sacrificial, and giving toward others in a way that was not possible before you got saved. This supernatural love is at the disposal of every Christian. When a person is born again, God puts the Holy Spirit in the believer to indwell them. The indwelling Holy Spirit produces the fruits of the Spirit in the life of every Christian. The leading fruit of the Spirit is love (Gal 5:28). The act of showing hospitable love toward others is evidence of true salvation. First John 3 says,

> We know that we have passed out of death into life, because we love the brethren. He who does not love abides in death. Everyone who hates his brother is a murderer; and you know that no murderer has eternal life abiding in him. We know love by this, that He laid down His life for us; and we ought to lay down our lives for the brethren. But whoever has the world's goods, and sees his brother in need and closes his heart against him, how does the love of God abide in him? Little children, let us not love with word or with tongue, but in deed and truth.

Verse 17 above is a sober warning. If you call yourself a Christian but you are unwilling to help those in need when you have the resources to do so, then John says it is questionable whether you are even a child of God. Because God has put His supernatural love in the heart of every genuine believer, we should welcome the idea of welcoming strangers in the name of Christ. Hospitality begins in the heart.

Ask God for Help

We all have weaknesses and blind spots (James 3:2). Those blind spots include selfishness, self-preservation, partiality, prejudice, or greed. All such sins can undermine the heart of hospitality. Being that we are all susceptible to these sins, we need to regularly go before God's throne of grace and mercy in prayer, and ask Him to search our hearts. Ask Him to expose any blind spots. Ask Him to use others around you that know you well to help expose your blind spots to ensure that you are not neglecting the biblical command to be hospitable to strangers (Prov 27:6). Remember David's prayer in Psalm 139, "Search me, O God, and know my heart; try me and know my anxious thoughts; and see if there be any hurtful way in me" (vv. 23-24). Ask God regularly to cultivate a hospitable attitude in yourself. Ask God to expose any residual selfishness or prejudice you may harbor that undermines fulfilling the mandate to be hospitable. God's Word says, "You do not have because you do not ask" (James 4:2). Jesus said, "Ask, and it will be given to you" (Matt 7:7). The Bible also says when we ask for anything according to His will then He will give it to us: "This is the confidence we have before Him, that if we ask anything according to His will, He hears us. And if we know that He hears us *in* whatever we ask, we know that we have the requests which we have asked from Him" (1 John 5:14-15). We need to be very specific when we pray. If you regularly plead with God to give you a hospitable attitude then He will answer that prayer.

Get Discipled
Observe those around you who are hospitable and learn from them. Jesus was the Master teacher. He taught His disciples by precept but also by practice. He told them, "Follow Me" (Matt 4:19). He wanted them to learn by observation, and they did learn as they followed Him, walked in His shadow, and observed His methods. They watched Him pray (Luke 9:18). They watched Him preach and teach (Matt 7:28-29). They watched Him serve (John 13). They watched Him extend kindness (Luke 17:11 ff.). They watched Him rebuke (Matt 23). Consequently, in time and thanks to His modeling, they would do the same (Acts 1:8). This is discipleship. If you are not good at being hospitable then find a mentor and get discipled in that area. Think of people in your church who are exemplary at hospitality, then talk with them, ask them questions, shadow them as they love strangers.

Remember God Owns Everything
Treat everything you own as though it belonged to God...because it does: "The earth is the LORD's, and all it contains" (Ps 24:1). The Bible says that every-thing we own was given to us by God as a gift. Paul asked, "What do you have that you did not receive?" (1 Cor

4:7). He meant that everything you possess and own was given to you by God as gift—your cash, your job, your car, your house, your food, your stocks, your cell phone—all of it. We are merely stewards of all that we have. When we truly come to realize that nothing ultimately belongs to us, then it will be much easier to share it with others. When was the last time you let someone use your car? The willingness to share, or give to others, is at the heart of hospitality. Paul teaches in Ephesians 4 that the reason Christians are to work hard and earn income is not only so they can pay their bills, but also so they can share with others in need (v. 28). If all you think about when you get your paycheck is padding your wallet, amassing your savings, stabilizing your security, accumulating more goods, or planning your vacation, and yet you don't give one thought as to how you can share your wealth with those in need, then you have an unbiblical view of money.

Be Deliberate

Be deliberate about welcoming guests to your church. Whether it is a Sunday school class, a Bible study in your home, the worship Service on Sunday, the prayer meeting mid-week or a special ministry off campus, always take the time to meet visitors, especially first-time visitors. Our church is not big nor well-known, but in our thirteen years of existence we have had first-time visitors almost every Sunday—believers, unbelievers, people new to the area, relatives just visiting family. We purpose to greet all of them and welcome them. We have greeters on Sunday welcoming folks as they come in. We make sure our greeters love people, especially strangers, and that they are warm and friendly. We take seriously the commands in the epistles that say, "Greet one another" (Rom 16:16; 1 Cor 16:20; 2 Cor 13:12; 1 Pet 5:14). We have a time after every Sunday service where visitors can meet with one of our elders and get their questions answered, get counsel, or even a prayer. We try to follow up with all our visitors by thanking them for coming via email or a phone call. We invite all our Sunday guests to come to our fellowship meal after the service, which has proven to be an ideal setting to get to know visitors and strangers better. Our people routinely invite visitors to lunch after the service.

Leaders Take the Lead

To nurture a culture of hospitality in the local church it needs to start with the leadership: the elders and pastors. We saw earlier that hospitality was a qualification required of elders. When the church leaders are graciously, winsomely, regularly living out hospitality and exhibiting a welcoming attitude toward visitors and strangers at the church, then the saints will follow in like manner. There is nothing worse than visiting a church as a first-time visitor, and instead of a warm welcome, all you get are strange stares and the cold shoulder, as all the regular attenders pretend not to see you as they treat you like a ghost...or the plague.

Sadly, many of us have visited a church like that. In such instances one feels like a trespasser who snuck over the fence at the local moose lodge or some elite country club, having no right to be among the privileged members. The worst example for me was when I was interviewing at a large Bible church to be their next preacher. They told me they had over 100 resumes come in from around the country and that I was in the top five for consideration. I then decided to visit the church incognito as a visitor to check out the church. To my disappointment, not one person greeted me, said hello, or even noticed me the entire ninety minutes I was there. They even had a greeting time at the beginning of the service. Hundreds of folks who were there that day simply chose to say "Hi" and greet only people they knew. I left at the end of the service, walking by several folks, rubbing shoulders with a few along the way, but not one person noticed me. A couple weeks later I was told, "The position has been filled." I was at peace.

That experience, and a few others I have had over the years at other churches, reminds me of James 2, the classic passage on corporate hospitality in the local church:

> My brethren, do not hold your faith in our glorious Lord Jesus Christ with *an attitude of* personal favoritism. For if a man comes into your assembly with a gold ring and dressed

in fine clothes, and there also comes in a poor man in dirty clothes, and you pay special attention to the one who is wearing the fine clothes, and say, "You sit here in a good place," and you say to the poor man, "You stand over there, or sit down by my footstool," have you not made distinctions among yourselves, and become judges with evil motives? Listen, my beloved brethren: did not God choose the poor of this world *to be* rich in faith and heirs of the kingdom which He promised to those who love Him? But you have dishonored the poor man. Is it not the rich who oppress you and personally drag you into court? Do they not blaspheme the fair name by which you have been called? If, however, you are fulfilling the royal law according to the Scripture, "YOU SHALL LOVE YOUR NEIGHBOR AS YOURSELF," you are doing well. But if you show partiality, you are committing sin *and* are convicted by the law as transgressors.

James says that if you show favoritism with visitors that is "evil" (v. 4) and "sin" (v. 9). Recently one of my seminary students shared with the class that he once attended a church that literally would not let people in the church if they were not dressed appropriately. Specifically, if the visitor of the day did not look "nice" or up to formal snuff, but rather was kind of dingy, shabby or seedy, then they could not join the others in corporate worship. That is evil and sin. Thank God for the example of Jesus who welcomed the downcast, ostracized, despised and even sinners (Luke 5:29-32).

Of all the people in the world who should be welcoming to strangers, it should be Christians. And the most loving place in the community should be the local church. As we remember and regularly practice the biblical principles listed above, then these two expectations can become a reality. And as a result, God will be pleased, the love of Christ will be put on display, strangers will be ministered to, and believers will be blessed.

6

A TESTIMONY ON HOSPITALITY

In this book we showed that being hospitable is a command from God to every Christian. Hospitality means to love and welcome strangers who have practical needs. This practical love flows from a heart of supernatural love that results from believing the gospel and possessing the indwelling Spirit who lives in every Christian. The Bible models this ministry of practical love from cover to cover. Jesus was the Master at modeling hospitality. We were reminded that Jesus said, "It is more blessed to give than to receive."

As with any biblical imperative, the goal is to implement and create godly habits of life—not just understand theoretical or theological truths. Our little church has been blessed by God with the gift of many saints who routinely practice biblical hospitality. The following is a testimony from one of our young couples who make hospitality a priority in their walk with Christ. I trust you will find it edifying and motivating as you pursue the practice of stranger love in your own life:

We love having people come over to our place. Here's how God has brought us to our convictions regarding hospitality and how practicing hospitality looks for our family. We pray you will be encouraged.

My wife's desire for practicing hospitality in an intentional way started soon after she was saved. She noticed that her friends would comment on how "hospitable" she was. As she grew in her faith and learned that she should be using her resources for God's glory, she began to plan more occasions to have people over in her home. She enjoyed hosting even more knowing it was from God and for God. She remembers thinking fondly of how the early church would break bread daily in their homes (Acts 2:46). One example of hospitality that she'll never forget was the time she was in Arizona, alone in a new place. One evening, at the end of her first visit to a church small group, as she was leaving the host's home she was told, "we eat dinner every night at 6:30pm…so just come over whenever." She was blown away by this generous and kind invitation from someone she had just met. Other examples she has been encouraged by were friends who hosted church-wide events regularly, friends who opened their home every Sunday afternoon with homemade popcorn, and friends who hosted travelers better than a 5-star hotel.

I have always enjoyed entertaining people as well, but it was after God saved me that He developed a desire to host as a means of edifying other believers and evangelizing the lost. During college my roommates and I enjoyed hosting Bible studies, prayer nights, and meals. I also benefited from many different church families who have opened their homes for meals, prayer, discipleship, and Bible studies. These experiences along with encouragement from my wife have helped me grow in practicing hospitality.

We have been recipients of much hospitality, first from God who welcomed us as sinners to Himself, and then from His people. Many godly examples have helped us grow in our convictions, individually and as a family. We are so thankful we can host together as a family now. Even though it has looked different in each season of life, whether we were single, married, or now with children, in a small home or big home, our desire has been the same: to be good stewards of the home and resources God has given us (Rom 11:36, Ps 24:1). We aim to be generous toward others and use what we have to bless others (1 Tim 6:17-19). Whether we are considering a new home or planning our current home's layout, we contemplate how it will accommodate large gatherings, visitors, or overnight guests.

With this mindset and God's blessing, we've had many opportunities to open our home, whether it was our 1-bedroom apartment or 4-bedroom house. One of the ways we've been able to use our home is hosting church events. It's been a blessing, joy, and privilege to be a part of the various ministries in this way. To get involved initially, we reached out and sought opportunities. Then, as God provided, we discussed them together before committing.

Practicing hospitality does have its challenges because we are sinful. In our selfishness we often think wrongly. We complain that hosting is tiring, think it's inconvenient, get upset that the baby's nap is being interrupted, or wish that we could keep all our resources for ourselves. We can also be discontent and wish our home were bigger, smaller, or cleaner. We may be tempted into thinking that we are too busy with work or our own family's activities.

Thank the Lord that He gives us grace to overcome all these challenges! We actively fight off wrong thoughts and replace them with true ones through His Word. We often need to encourage one another to think rightly through God's Word. His Word reminds us to love God with all our heart, soul, mind, and strength, and to love our neighbor as ourselves (Mark 12:30-31), to be content with what we have (Phil 4:12), to consider others first (Phil 2:3), to remember that it is better to give than to receive (Acts 20:35), to serve by His strength and for His glory (1 Pet 4:11), to lay up treasures in heaven and not on earth (Matt 6:19-21), to not neglect meeting together (Heb 10:25), to love our brothers with sincerity (Rom 12:9-10), to serve one another with zeal (Rom 12:11), to contribute to the needs of other believers (Rom 12:13), and to show hospitality (Rom 12:13).

We also need to pray for help to serve with a glad and generous heart. God is faithful and gives us strength, brings help from others, and gives us humility to be okay with serving simple meals and using paper plates and plastic utensils. Our place isn't always clean, and with young children, we sometimes need to get creative with cooking and ask our guests to be gracious with us.

God has not only helped us through these challenges but He's also blessed us immensely through each hosting opportunity. There is so much joy in seeing people meet new people, deepen relationships, serve and encourage each other, evangelize non-believers, and reconnect. In terms of ministry, opening our home is a way we can serve and love others. Practically, hosting enables us to have fellowship with others and it sometimes challenges our cooking skills! Our marriage has been blessed because when we host we practice and fine-tune our communication skills and it is also something fun that we can work on together. Our home is warmer, kept cleaner, and utilized fuller when we have people over, including strangers. It's wonderful to see so much ministry happening in our home!

All Christians should practice hospitality (Rom 12:13, 1 Pet 4:9, Heb 13:2). You can practice hospitality regardless of the size or cleanliness of your home. Whether you host one person or 100, you are practicing hospitality. We should all ask God for opportunities to serve and minister to others with the homes and material things that we've been graciously given by the Creator and Giver of all things.

Opening our homes helps us edify the church body and evangelize the lost. It sets us apart from our society that glorifies individualism and shuns strangers. May Christians be lights in this dark world through opening our hearts and homes to people for God's glory.

NOTES

Chapter 1—What is Biblical Hospitality?

1. Robert K. Barnhart, ed., *Chambers Dictionary of Etymology* (Chambers Harrap Publishers: New York, 1988), 492.

2. *Chambers Dictionary*, 492.

3. D. Edmond Hiebert, *1 Peter*, BMH Books: Winona Lake, Indiana, 1992, 273.

Chapter 2—Hospitality in the Old Testament

1. *Encyclopaedia Judaica*, vol. 8 (Keter Publishing House, Jerusalem, Israel 1971), 1030.

2. *Encylcopaedia Judaica*, 8:1031.

Chapter 3—Jesus and Hospitality

1. John MacArthur, *The MacArthur New Testament Commentary: Luke 1-5*, (Chicago: Moody, 2009), 149-50.

2. John MacArthur, *The MacArthur New Testament Commentary: Matthew 8-15*, (Moody, 1987), 22.

ABOUT THE AUTHOR

Rev. Cliff McManis has been in pastoral ministry since 1989. He is a graduate of The Master's University and The Master's Seminary. He is the author of *Christian Living Beyond Belief*, *Apologetics by the Book*, *The Biblically-Driven Church*, *What the Bible Says About Depression* and editor and contributing author of *Rescued by Grace*. Pastor McManis is also a professor and board member of the Cornerstone Bible College and Seminary in Vallejo, CA. He has served in churches in southern California, Utah, Texas, and the San Francisco Bay Area, and is currently pastor-teacher at Creekside Bible Church in Cupertino, California. He and his family currently reside in Northern California.

ABOUT WITH ALL WISDOM

With All Wisdom is the Christian media creation ministry located in Cupertino, CA. We started this publishing ministry out of the simple desire to serve the local body with substantive biblical resources for the sake of our people's growth and spiritual maturity.

But we also believe that book publishing, like any other Christian ministry, should first and foremost be under the supervision and accountability of the local church. While we are grateful for and will continue to support the many excellent traditional publishers available today—our shelves are full of the books they have produced—we also believe that the best place to develop solid, life-giving theology and biblical instruction is within the local church.

With All Wisdom is also unique because we offer our books at a very low cost. We strive for excellence in our writing and seek to provide a high-quality product to our readers. Our editorial team is comprised of men and women who are highly trained and excellent in their craft. But since we are able to avoid the high overhead costs that are typically incurred by traditional publishers, we are able to pass significant savings on to you. The result is a growing collection of books that are substantive, readable, and affordable.

In order to best serve various spiritual and theological needs of the body of Christ, we have developed three distinct lines of books. **Big Truth | little books**® provides readers with accessible, manageable works on theology, Christian living, and important church and social issues in a format that is easy to read and easy to finish. Our **Equip Series** is aimed at Christians who desire to delve a little deeper into doctrine and practical matters of the faith. Our **Foundations Series** is our academic line in which we seek to contribute to the contemporary theological discussion by combining pastoral perspective with rigorous scholarship.

OTHER TITLES FROM WITH ALL WISDOM PUBLICATIONS

Please visit us at WithAllWisdom.org to learn more about these titles

BIG TRUTH little books®
What the Bible Says About Gray Areas
Cliff McManis

Faith: The Gift of God
Cliff McManis

How to Pray for Your Pastor
Derek Brown

The Problem of Evil
Cliff McManis

What the Bible Says About Government
Cliff McManis

God Defines and Defends Marriage
Cliff McManis

Protecting the Flock: The Priority of Church Membership
Cliff McManis

What the Bible Says About Confrontation
Cliff McManis

*Fellowship with God: A Guide to Bible Reading,
Meditation, and Prayer*
Derek Brown

Equip
*The Biblically-Driven Church:
How Jesus Builds His Body*
Cliff McManis

*God's Glorious Story:
The Truth of What It's All About*
Colin Eakin

*Strong and Courageous: The Character and Calling of
Mature Manhood*
Derek Brown

*The Gospel, the Church, and Homosexuality: How the
Gospel is Still the Power of God for
Redemption and Transformation*
Edited by Michael Sanelli and Derek Brown

Foundations
Apologetics by the Book
Cliff McManis

www.ingramcontent.com/pod-product-compliance
Lightning Source LLC
Chambersburg PA
CBHW020507030426
42337CB00011B/271

how the spiritual writings I read have affected my life and helped to shape my spiritual beliefs and values.

I wish to thank the authors and acknowledge the work of both the ancient masters and current writers for their important contributions to my spiritual development.

Introduction

An Echo in the Woods

I hear a distant voice calling.
Like an echo in the woods.

I pay no attention
But it keeps coming back
Like a poem's refrain.

It's telling me there is *more*.
That there is more than what I see all
around me.

More to be done than simply satisfy my
own selfish needs.

It's telling me that I am so much more than
this body of mine.

That I am so much more than my puny
mind allows me to believe.

The voice is telling me that I have infinite potential and great power as yet untapped.

It calls me to a more noble
And meaningful existence.

An echo in the woods...
Do you hear it?

❀ ❀ ❀

If you answered "yes" to the question above, then this book may help to fill that void. What is written here will have appeal to those who already acknowledge their spirituality as well as those who are not really sure what it means to be a spiritual person. In fact, the idea or feeling that there is *more* may well be the central theme of this book.

This book is not written from the perspective of religion. Instead, it explores and seeks to identify fundamental, and universal qualities of spirituality, and what gives life meaning.

A variety of written forms are used in this exploration such as essays, verse, and dialogues. The writing style is often more poetic than narrative adding a dimension of beauty and metaphor while at the same time expressing the message in simple terms that are easily understood and internalized.

Those who do not identify with or participate in any religion are one of the fastest growing groups in the U.S. Its members include young and old, persons who grew up without religion in the home, as well as others who for a variety of reasons chose to discontinue practice of the religion of their upbringing. Those in the latter category have not necessarily abandoned religion or a belief in God. Many, like me, have instead set out to learn about all of the major world religions with the aim of mining for universal spiritual truths, ways of living, and habits of mind that resonate with them.

Some of those who grew up without religion may at some point in their life begin to feel a

vague yearning for more in life than consumerism can provide. As implied in the verse above,
many do not know where to look, or for what
exactly it is that they are searching. The writing
in this book will provide some answers.

Chapter One

The Revelation of More

...That indescribable feeling that there is more to life than work, family, and consumerism. Something is missing that you intuitively know would bring greater joy, happiness, and fulfillment to your life.

There are two dimensions to this feeling that there is more. One is that we sense that there is more to us than our body and mind—something abstract, mysterious, even mystical. I believe it to be our spirit. Consider the following essay.

We Exist in the Ethereal Spaces Between the Atoms

We were created in spirit and will remain so forever more. Our spiritual existence does not stop or go into abeyance during the brief periods when we are clothed with a physical body. We may lose touch with our spirit-self from time to time, stupefied by the many distractions of the physical world.

But in the background, out of the din, our spirit cries out for expression. The challenge is to have the presence of mind and *desire* to hear it.

Our spirit calls to us with the sweet, soft voice of a lover, to remind us that we exist in the ethereal spaces *between* the atoms of the physical world. We are merely passersby and should consider what spiritual legacy we wish to create in the physical world, because that is the only thing that will follow us when it is time to move on.

While all that is composed eventually will be decomposed, our spirits will continue to exist as a part of our everlasting Creator. Just as He has always existed and always will, so shall we.

The other facet of *more* is the yearning for greater happiness and meaning in our lives that goes beyond fulfilling one's material needs. The essay below addresses many of the issues that underlie the search for this seemingly elusive higher dimension of existence.

❧ ❧ ❧

In this day and age, we live in a world that focuses on, and values, material things rather than the spiritual qualities of existence. This has led to the widespread rise of ignoble qualities of personality in many people such as pride, ego, greed, selfishness, narcissism, and self-aggrandizement. Sadly, it appears that a surprising number of people have not known any other way to live.

The pursuit of happiness leads far too many people down countless blind alleys and confusing twists and turns. Just when we think we have found the key, it vanishes leaving us once again feeling empty and unfulfilled.

Placing a high value on material things and living a material lifestyle naturally leads one to seek happiness from material things. A common misconception is that if I had a new car, or could buy a house, or had more money, or could find the love of my life, or get my dream job, etc. then I would finally be happy and fulfilled.

Each of us has proven this approach and vision of happiness to be false. Accumulation of worldly possessions does not bring genuine, lasting happiness.

Another aspect of this that many people do not realize is that wanting and craving things we do not have are what lead to *un*happiness. It is the wanting itself that brings discontent, not the lack of things desired.

Nevertheless, for many of us, it is easier to identify worldly things and circumstances that might make us happy, rather than doing the soul-searching needed to understand how personal happiness can be nurtured.

Each of us is responsible for our own happiness. It cannot be given to us by some thing or someone else.

That said, then how does one find true happiness? What exactly does it mean to be truly happy? I believe that true happiness can only be found within ourselves and exists independent of the world around us. Happiness is a reflection of the state of our spirit-selves. Those who have achieved harmony between spirit, mind, and body have found the key to happiness.

I believe that happiness is a natural result of spiritual fulfillment. Nothing brings a greater sense of satisfaction and purpose than expression of our spirit through love, compassion, and helping others. Reflecting on this, we all know it is true. Loving and helping others brings jubilation like nothing else can. Therefore, we all know that this is the key to deep and meaningful happiness.

The challenge we all face is keeping the spiritual perspective of happiness always foremost in our minds. We must constantly strive to re-order our lives, values, and priorities to pursue spiritual fulfillment and progression, rather than worldly pleasures, satisfaction, and status.

Deep inside we all know the right path for the pursuit of happiness. How many of us can muster the conviction and determination we need to take and stay on that path?

❀   ❀   ❀

In the dialogue below between teacher and student, the question of the meaning of life is explored.

"Teacher, why am I here?" I asked.

"You are here to change the world," the teacher replied in a matter-of-fact tone.

Taken aback I asked, "How can I change the world when I am only *one* among *billions?*"

"Ah, but you are not alone in this," he said. There are many like you around the world seeking to expand their spiritual awareness. There are even more who seek meaning for their lives, but are not yet spiritually aware."

"But teacher, what is it that gives life meaning, or perhaps I should say: what is the meaning of life?" I wondered.

He smiled as a parent might to a child's simple-minded question and replied, "There are some who seek meaning by pursuing a career. Others seek meaning through their family life. Still others seek meaning through devotion to their religion, but the answer is much more basic than these things."

"I can see where one could get some measure of satisfaction and fulfillment from each of these," I said.

"Yes, but there is something more fundamental that brings meaning to these and all human endeavors," replied the teacher.

Not understanding where the teacher was going with this, I asked, "What is more basic than making one's way in the world, love of family, and devotion to God?" When I heard his answer, I felt as if I were indeed a naive child again.

He said, "You must understand that all of the children of Earth have kinship with one another. All of humanity arose from one and the same God the Father. Consequently, you are expected to give all persons you meet the same love and compassion that you would to your own parents, siblings, children, etc. It is helping and serving others that is most fulfilling and that gives life its true meaning."

Trying to grasp a deeper understanding of what the teacher was saying, I declared, "So what you are saying is that love and compassion should underlie and guide all human interactions."

"Yes, that is why you are here! That is how you will change the world! That is your life's purpose!" he said. "This is the lesson that humanity must learn!"

❀   ❀   ❀

What the teacher is saying is that there is a whole other dimension to our existence that for most of us is locked away deep inside and essentially unknown to us. I wrote the verse below the summer after graduating from college. I wrote it in the context of a relationship with a young woman and therefore thought it was about her. It was not until some forty years later that I realized that the poem was actually about *me*. In fact, its message is applicable to the vast majority of us. It likens our spirituality to rays of light that we too often shut away. And having done so, we live much of our lives unaware of our spirit-selves.

The Light Inside You

For only a few fleeting moments
Have I felt the warm light of you—
Of what is inside of you.

Those moments were like rays of light
Peeking through the cracks of a door
In a dark room.

I am in the darkness alone,
Longing to know
What lies on the other side of the door.
Yearning to feel the touch
Of the warm and beautiful
Light that lies there.

But the door is locked,
The key to its opening
Unknown to me.

So I will wait—
Yes, wait patiently
For the next beam of light
To spill through the cracks.

Longing to know
To understand
To embrace
The wonderful light
That shines inside of you.

It is my belief that no matter who you are, what kind of a person you are, or what kind of life you live, there have been moments when your spirit was able to squeeze through the cracks in the walls you may have built around yourself. The fortresses we build to protect ourselves are always flawed and conquerable from within and without.

Our spirit-selves, that some of us try to hold captive in the darkness of our fears, doubt, and insecurities, yearn—no, demand expression. No matter how hard you try to cling to the material world and deny your spirituality, your spirit will always seek to show you a better way.

If you accept the notion that your spirit is what gives life and your spirit-self is the real you, then you can see that your spirit must be allowed to express itself. Otherwise are you really alive?

I believe that we are all spiritual beings. We, and those around us, look for evidence of this in us and in themselves. They are searching for the warm and beautiful light emanating from others and hope to find within themselves. Perhaps we do not realize that all we have to do is open the door, even if only a crack at first.

This next dialogue uses the metaphor of the spirit-self as our faithful and ever present companion in life ready to lead us out of darkness. Once we acknowledge that we are spiritual beings, everything changes and we begin to see life as a spiritual progression through eternity rather than a short temporal existence.

My Companion and Me

"Are you feeling lost and downhearted? Come, take my hand and follow me. We have been strangers for too long. Do not be afraid."

"Where are we going," I asked?

"We are going where you have always yearned to go. Come I will show you the way. The path we will walk together can be difficult, but the destination is well worth it."

"This is too hard. I don't think I can do it."

"Of course you can! Focus on the light up ahead. It will give you strength. Don't you see how it gets brighter the farther we go?"

"I didn't realize how we were emerging from such a dark place. As I look back down the path from where we came, I see that it fades into total darkness. I did not know how lost and confused I was back there."

"We still have a long way to go, but I will be with you every step of the way. Just don't let go of my hand or lose sight of the expanding light ahead."

"The farther we go, the closer I feel to you."

"I have always been a part of you waiting for you to take notice. Now that you have acknowledged me, we can continue the journey truly as one—fearless with great strength and conviction."

✿   ✿   ✿

The spiritual perspective of life is very different from, and in many ways diametrically opposed to, the material life. The following verse illustrates perception of the world through the eyes of our spirit.

With Spirit Eyes I See

With spirit eyes I see you...

With spirit eyes I see you and I are kindred spirits.

With spirit eyes I see we are all connected parts of a whole.

With spirit eyes I see many paths leading to higher levels of spiritual awareness.

With spirit eyes I see a powerful being unaware of its spirit-self.

With spirit eyes I see your spirit body (the real you)—so beautiful and perfect.

With spirit eyes I see your potential for unconditional love for all living things.

With spirit eyes I see me...

With spirit eyes I clearly see and understand my transgressions.

With spirit eyes I see that my suffering can lead to redemption and greater awareness.

With spirit eyes I see the invisible ones always close at hand to help me.

With spirit eyes I see the beautiful light and love that radiates from them.

With spirit eyes I see that my purpose is to serve. With spirit eyes I see that this is what gives life meaning.

Each of us has the potential to see the world through our spirit eyes. It is a choice we can make, but one that must come from purity of intent. That is, a desire to not only see as spirit, but to also live life according to what spirit shows us.

Our mind governs our perceptions of the world and how we react to it. I believe that the mind has two aspects or qualities: *spiritual and intellectual*. We are all familiar with the intellectual mind. It is responsible for processes like reasoning, judgment, analysis, calculation, ego, desire, and other mundane faculties. I envision the spiritual mind engaging in activities such as creativity, intuition, and psychic abilities.

The two aspects of mind likely operate on different planes of consciousness. The intellectual mind (IM) focuses on the physical world, while the spiritual mind (SM) searches for meaning, and communion with God.

Worldly knowledge is acquired by the IM through study and investigation of measurable quantities. Spiritual knowledge can be obtained to some extent by study also. However, oftentimes, the most profound spiritual knowledge comes to us without active searching or any effort on our part except having an open mind and a desire to come closer to God.

Sometimes spiritual knowledge defies logic and ordinary understanding. It can come to us with an inexplicable certainty in its truth, while at the same time we do not how we know it or from where the knowledge came to us.

The two minds look at the world and existence quite differently. The IM primarily sees the here and now, while the SM senses there is much more to existence.

Dominance by the IM may lead one to deny or overlook their spiritual nature. It may also lead one to question the existence of God or a Creator, as the IM favors (or perhaps requires) measurement and proof over intuition and faith.

In contrast, the SM cares little about the material aspects of existence favoring instead expression of itself through inspiration, creativity, psychic connection, and emotions such as love and compassion.

How do the two aspects of mind reconcile with one another? The IM is essential in order for us to function in the material world. The SM brings meaning to the activities of the IM. The spiritual qualities of mentality moderate and guide the IM toward applications of its faculties that will be spiritually fulfilling and serve the greater good. I believe that a key element of our spiritual progression and evolution is for the SM to achieve dominance over the IM.

As human beings it is our nature to always seek more. But our desire for more is really a search for meaning and purpose, not for material wealth or status. Those who seek only material things will not find lasting happiness. While those who seek meaning eventually will hear their spirit's call and life's secret will be revealed to them.

Chapter Two

The Spiritual Gift of Love

Spirit's Answer to my Prayer

...And Spirit told me: "Love and compassion are not mental processes; rather, they are an expression of the spirit. Follow your heart and let them flow freely without thought, fear, or any other product of the mind. Do what comes naturally and have faith that you are being guided. Be of the conviction that actions to help others compelled by the expression of love and compassion (of the spirit) always will be healing and nurturing to the soul of the recipient."

The Quintessence of Life

What is the quintessence of life—that magical elixir from which all life arose and which fills it with jubilation? What is the highest, most noble element that is pervasive throughout the heavenly realms?

I believe that *love* is the fundamental component of all planes of existence. Love is an uncreated *spiritual quality* that is a healing, nurturing, fulfilling, and guiding force. It is the primordial element from which we arose and to which we shall return.

Divine love comes from without (from God and the holy spirits that serve him) and it comes from within (from the divinity of our spirit-selves). It is all encompassing and encompassed by all.

Love is the greatest of all commandments. The purpose of our journeys through the millennia is, in large part, to come to understand that we are capable of unconditional love for all things, and once realized, to radiate that love through expression of our spirit-selves.

After many lifetimes our spirit will emerge to full expression and our love for all things truly will have no bounds or conditions. When that happens, our Earth journeys may well end returning our spirit to its most basic existence— one that simply radiates divine love forever and ever.

Love transcends matter, space, and time. It is foremost among the spiritual mysteries, and a treasured gift from God that is meant to be shared with all.

❋   ❋   ❋

Some time ago, prior to writing on the quintessence of life, the question below popped into my head and haunted me for days. I kept repeating the question over and over in my mind like I sometimes do when I am trying to remember something or solve a problem. Each time I did so, I felt twinges of emotion that begged for expression and understanding. I found myself searching for an answer to the question that went beyond the sort of worldly aspects of what we call "heart."

Finally, the constant nagging of this question forced me to sit down at the computer and wait quietly for an answer. Soon, the words started to flow and the verse below was born.

To What Doth My Heart Hearken?

To what doth my heart hearken?
This is the question that haunts me in every waking moment.

Though it beats in my chest, my heart seems somehow abstract and transcendent.
It calls to me with sweet refrain.

And like the Siren my heart's song draws me in a new direction.

But not to destruction; rather, to new meaning and purpose.

I do not want to resist; the melody is too beautiful.

The notes hit a chord that makes my spirit sing.

I am compelled to seek the source of this wondrous beauty

That I may come to know it in its fullness.

"What would you have me do," I ask?

The answer came swiftly and powerfully in a single word

That resonated in the essence of my being—"LOVE!"

❀   ❀   ❀

I think that by "heart" we intuitively (yet perhaps unwittingly) mean *spirit*. I believe that love, charitable acts, artistic talents, etc. are expressions of the spirit—of our divine selves. Consequently, these are actions that we find most satisfying and fulfilling.

Perhaps the most common reference to the heart is that it is the source of a person's love. What is suggested here is that love comes from our spirit. I would go further to say that love is the *hallmark* of spiritual expression. It is the essence of our divine nature. We are only truly happy when we allow our love to flow, but not just for spouse and family; rather, for all people and all of creation. Listen to your heart's (your spirit's) sweet refrain!

❈   ❈   ❈

If we are all children of God, then perhaps we have inherited certain divine qualities. If this is true, then how is my divine-self revealed? The following provides an example.

Charity that comes from the heart is an act of love and compassion where the spirit reveals itself in all of its divine glory. It raises us up ever so slightly so that our feet seem to lose touch with the ground, if only briefly. With each charitable act, a wave of happiness and fulfillment washes over us and for those few moments, we understand the meaning and purpose of life. We realize that our joy comes from giving of ourselves—our spirit-selves—to others.

But too often these moments are fleeting. When our feet touch the ground again, we find ourselves longing to soar once more, free of the constraints, obligations, and selfish desires of the physical life. But it is not our time to fly away just yet. We must prove ourselves worthy of wings!

How is My Divine Self Revealed?

I believe that the divine self is manifested by the spirit and that, as indicated above, love and compassion are spiritual attributes. Therefore, one way in which we reveal our divinity is by expression of love and compassion for all things.

Compassion is not an attribute exclusive to people of religious faith. In fact, it did not originate in religion; rather, it is an aspect of our in-born divine nature. It is an attribute of *humanity*. Everyone has it, but we get lost from time to time on our life path and stray from our inherent loving and generous nature. What is important is that we recognize that the spiritual gifts of love and compassion are at the core of our being; that when we express these qualities, we are revealing our divinity to ourselves and to those whose lives we touch.

Nothing is more rewarding or more important in life than sharing these spiritual gifts with others. What is important in the pursuit of meaning in our lives is that we all aspire and strive to express our divinity in various ways on a daily basis. It is through these actions that our divine-self is revealed.

Now let's turn to a more mundane discussion of the role of love in our everyday lives. It seems everyone is obsessed with looking for love these days, whether it be a physical hook-up or the search for a soul mate. Either way the focus is on one's self. Most of us have this backwards. We should be *giving* love to those all around us. This will, in turn, attract love to us.

I believe that love is a form of spiritual energy that is independent of biology and worldly context. Love as spiritual energy may be heralded by that sense of a mutual connection between people. It is a spiritual connection not a physical one. This is what we look for in a mate and find in our family and best friends. When will we learn to go beyond the physical and start to listen to what our spirit tells us?

Restricting our love to spouse, family, and friends is not sufficient for spiritual progression and does not fulfill our divine capacity and responsibility to love broadly. Radiating our divine love to all we encounter is the ultimate expression of our spirit and spirituality.

We have all heard the cliché "Only love can save the world." This is one of those truths that sadly will remain a cliché until we begin to take it seriously and apply it globally in our everyday lives. If you want to change the world your love has to flow out *away* from yourself to everyone around you including total strangers.

I acknowledge that this is not always easy, especially when someone is being unmanageable. But we need to try to not react, and simply radiate love and kindness. Sometimes this will disarm the one acting up; sometimes it will not. Nevertheless, we need to make the effort, because the intent behind actions is what they will be measured against in the spiritual realms. If your genuine intent was to give love freely and it was rejected, you still benefit spiritually from your efforts. You will acquire spiritual capital that will help you going forward.

You may wonder how can loving globally change the world. When people see the effect your loving ways have on them and others, some will want to give the same happiness to people they encounter and feel the joy and fulfillment that they see in you.

As we move through our day, we need to make an effort to see beyond ourselves, and our own selfish needs and desires. We need to be nice to people and show kindness to others, even if they are being a bit difficult.

All of us should take the time to give serious thought to what the world would be like if the majority focused on helping others, rather than pursuing their own fame, fortune, and love life. After thinking about this, you may conclude that love can indeed save the world.

I said that radiating our divine love to all we encounter is the ultimate expression of our spirit and spirituality. I believe that each of us has a spiritual kinship with all members of the human race. This is summed up by the world view: **one God, one people**. When internalized, this concept is transformative on so many levels.

Insomuch as we are all children of the one true God, we are all kindred spirits with sameness perhaps likened to identical twins. In spirit form, we all "look" alike, and when first born as spirit, we all have the same potential for spiritual development. In spirit form, free of the physical body, all distinctions of race, ethnicity, national origin, gender, socioeconomic status, and so forth disappear. Therefore, we must learn to look past the body and see each other as spirit family members.

Each of our spirit kin, as in any family, has taken a different life path that we have neither walked nor seen what they have seen. Each path is different, presents different challenges, and affects each individual differently. Therefore, we need to be kind and patient with one another and not make assumptions or judgments.

If we genuinely understood our spiritual kinship, then we would care for all people as we care for our husbands, wives, children, and so forth. We would never allow anyone to be cold, hungry, or thirsty. Our love for our spirit kin would compel us to raise others up and fulfill their needs without hesitation or thought about ourselves.

One God, one people—I believe that all of humanity has a spiritual kinship. The challenge is not so much to come to this realization, but rather to live in a manner that reflects such a belief.

Chapter Three

So You Say You are Spiritual...

What does it mean to be a spiritual person? What is spiritual awareness?

In my view, there are a few basic attributes seen in all spiritual persons. First, they are aware that they have a spirit and that the spirit is what gives them life. It is behind their life force and it can guide and influence their thoughts and actions toward a life of goodness.

Having made the realization that we are composed of body and spirit, then one is usually compelled to explore and understand the fundamental nature of spirituality. This is essential because being spiritual is a way of living and a way of viewing the universe, the world, our place in them, and the meaning of life. Spirituality can arise and thrive within or without structured religion.

Once we come to truly understand that we are spiritual beings, everything changes. One of the changes is that we begin to move away from the material aspects of life and seek to understand the nonmaterial qualities of existence. Our focus shifts away from things and self-serving behaviors and thoughts to unselfish concern for the well-being of all living things. This is a major paradigm shift in world view for most people, especially in the years leading up to mid-life.

Once one acknowledges the presence of their spirit-self, the journey to discover what it means to be spiritual and to live the life of spirit begins. My hope and prayer is that it will come early in life for as many as possible so that the joy, happiness, and fulfillment it brings can be enjoyed for many years ahead.

Let's delve deeper into this notion of what it means to be spiritual. This next essay examines the relationship between spirit, body, and our creator.

Spirituality as a State of Being

I get the impression that much of the general public does not understand what it means to be spiritual. This appears to be the case with a surprising number of people regardless of whether or not they are members of a particular religion.

Those who have drifted away from organized religion often say that they are "spiritual" when asked about their religious affiliation. This is a convenient way to defuse the question and avoid further discussion. However, should they be pressed to explain what they mean, they often respond with something about being in touch with nature or something similar.

Spirituality is a very serious and deep subject that needs to be understood because it is an integral, critical part of our existence. Not everyone expresses their spirituality and, as a consequence, they are unable to live a truly happy and fulfilled life.

I believe that spirituality is a state of being and a way of living. It is an expression of the spirit-self in everyday life. It is the certainty of the presence of God in us and all of creation. It is recognition of our divine self as a part of our Creator. It is the realization that we are an integral part of God, not a dissociated remnant. This knowledge brings with it great responsibility.

The fact that we can exist in physical and spirit form at the same time may seem a contradiction. What is not understood by many is that our true existence is one of spirit. The body is like a garment the spirit wears for a short time that will be shed when it is no longer needed. It is a means by which we materialize in the physical world to engage in learning and attend to our life lessons.

But in putting on the garment, many things are hidden from us. We may lose sight of the spirit beneath the clothing. We may lose touch with our divinity hidden behind the shroud of our physicality. Looking in from the outside, we strain to see the bits of light that penetrate the fabric. Oftentimes, all we can see is waves of subdued light and shadows of what is on the other side. Our spirituality lies there beckoning us like a distant memory we struggle to recall.

Spirituality is a state of being, knowing, and living. It is an expansion of consciousness that sees beyond the body and the self. It is awareness that all things are a part of God and deserving of our love and respect.

If we are integral to our creator, then we have the qualities and potential of God for infinite love. This means we are imbued with the qualities of love and compassion for all living things. These are at the core of our divine nature, and spirituality cannot exist without their expression.

Thus, to understand and express our spirituality, we must find a way to express our divine nature in our everyday lives through our actions and how we live our lives.

❀   ❀   ❀

It is so easy to get caught up in focusing on our internal spiritual communion when in fact we should be focusing on everything all around us. A life of goodness must be all encompassing.

We must remind ourselves that while spirituality is found in part through internal reflection, it goes beyond self. It is not just a personal evolution. It is also making a connection with all of creation. It is about truly caring for (all) others, all living things, the planet, and so forth. With that care comes a sense of responsibility for the welfare of all these things.

I realize that I will not be fully developed spiritually until I can consistently do that. By directing my awareness on people and things outside of myself, I draw forth the divinity inside me that I want so much to express and experience.

As more and more of us direct our awareness and caring outside ourselves, we join together in a spiritual evolution of the human race. I believe this is our true calling. This is our common path to the highest realms of spiritual existence.

Spiritual awareness goes beyond a belief in God and the simple realization that we are spiritual beings. As noted in this next essay, it brings with it greater responsibility.

What is Spiritual Awareness?

Perhaps the most common and basic concept of spiritual awareness is simply an awareness of, belief in, or faith in a higher being.

I see faith as a doorway or threshold through which most people must pass in order to begin a path to spiritual awareness. There are exceptions to this, but for most of us faith in God is a necessary first step.

Those with spiritual awareness see the world very differently. They see God in everything around them. They feel his presence every minute of every day. They constantly give Him thanks and praise, and they make a very conscious effort to live a life of goodness. They hold themselves accountable for their mistakes, wrongdoing, and transgressions, and they have genuine repentance.

Living a spiritually aware life may be a major change in world view for many. Nevertheless, once having found the doorway to a spiritual life, do not be afraid to pass through. Keep an open mind and be prepared to make sacrifices and take on new responsibilities inherent in the knowledge you will receive.

While spiritual awareness typically begins with a belief in God, it is not a belief; *it is an experience*. As one's spiritual awareness expands beyond basic belief, things happen. One begins to have inspirations and revelations. New knowledge and understanding blossom within us. Sometimes knowledge we already had springs forth with a new perspective, or takes on a deeper meaning and significance. This new meaning sometimes compels us to take action of some sort.

Expanding spiritual awareness and knowledge often bring with them new responsibilities that may require personal sacrifices. An example from my own spiritual evolution was taking the position that the inhumane and cruel practices associated with raising animals in large numbers for food is wrong. This grew out of my expanding spiritual understanding of how all life forms are interconnected with each other and with God. I subsequently learned that the methods used to raise livestock also exploit and destroy the environment and make a major contribution to climate change.

I took responsibility for this revelation by committing to vegetarianism and I am now a staunch supporter of animal's rights. As one acquires more spiritual knowledge, one must adapt their thinking and behavior to reflect that knowledge. This is why I refer to spirituality as a developmental or evolutionary process.

To experience a more expansive spiritual awareness, we must truly open our minds and put aside any preconceived notions and prejudices. If we want to experience deeper levels of spiritual awareness, all we need do is ask, but we must be willing to change in response to the spiritual knowledge and understanding we receive.

Spiritual knowledge may be received or obtained in a variety of ways. This next article describes a special channel or process through which revelation may come to some people.

The Spiritual Experience of Knowing

What is the spiritual experience of "knowing" and how does it differ from other means by which we receive spiritual knowledge? I will try to answer these questions based on my own spiritual experiences. It is an event that may be difficult to grasp through description, and for some, difficult to believe without experiencing it themselves.

The spiritual type of knowing discussed here does not refer to factual knowledge, languages, or memory. Rather, as used here, it refers to an inexplicable revelation of spiritual knowledge of which one suddenly somehow *knows* with *absolute certainty*.

The knowing may take place in a brief, spontaneous altered state of consciousness, or simply by an abrupt, strong flood of thought. Either mode is sure to get one's attention. There will be no doubt that something extraordinary has occurred. The knowledge given in this manner may be previously unknown to the recipient, or it may involve something of which the recipient had prior knowledge, but which had not yet taken deep root in their spiritual awareness.

A characteristic aspect of this type of knowing is that it is unexpected, and sometimes powerful and overwhelming. It is a spiritual experience unlike anything you may have witnessed before.

This is in contrast to knowledge and beliefs that we get from scripture or other religious texts. Knowledge acquired in these ways may seem somewhat abstract, and through faith leads to intentional commitments that we make regarding religious and spiritual matters. That is not to say that spiritual experience cannot arise from foundations of faith, but rather faith and belief are not experiences in, and of themselves.

For example, one may have faith and believe that there is a God, accepting His existence as a concept. Whereas, a knowing would be to palpably *experience* His presence and qualities in an altered state of awareness.

In my book, *Building a Bridge between Two Worlds*, I describe some of my spiritual experiences of knowing. Each one was transformative and together they have changed the way I live, think, and view the world. They provided much of the impetus for the writing found in this book.

The experience of knowing is not something that one can willfully create. One must be spiritually ready to receive the knowledge it brings. A knowing is a spontaneous event for which the factors or circumstances needed for its occurrence are largely unknown. It is my belief that if one has an open mind concerning spirituality, a genuine desire for spiritual truth, and strives for purity of heart that they may become fertile ground for the spiritual experience of knowing.

This next essay examines the confluence of the spirit being with the physical being. How might this strange union work? How can two very different forms of being whose natural tendencies are so opposite compromise, and not just coexist, but work together for the higher good?

Harmony between Spirit, Mind, and Body

It seems to me that one of the goals as a spiritual person is to achieve harmony between the spirit, mind, and body. Here, I would define harmony as congruity between these three aspects of being. All three are integral parts of our existence, and as such interact with, and influence one another.

I think congruity is a key word here. In order for there to be harmony, the mind must be aware of the spirit and understand the nature, meaning, and purpose of a spiritual life. The mind must also be committed to a life of goodness and virtue. The body finds congruity by cultivating good health to fully support expression of the mind and spirit through outward action.

The state of the mind determines the extent to which the spirit is able to express itself. If the mind is at peace, open, and seeks spiritual awareness, it will come. When this happens, the mind is compelled to seek outlets for expression of the spirit-self. There is a transformation in one's motives, intent, and desire.

When harmony is achieved, love and compassion for all things dominates the person's world view. One's thoughts are outwardly directed toward the needs of others. There is a strong desire to serve God and humanity, and material things become relatively unimportant. Expression of the spirit energizes mind and body bringing feelings of happiness and well-being.

❀ ❀ ❀

Let's shift gears to discuss a practical matter that is perhaps one of the greatest barriers to becoming a spiritual person. As we all know, there are some serious challenges we must face in order to develop and maintain our spiritual outlook on life. Most outstanding among them is the ego. Many spiritual figures and writers over the ages have addressed this issue from Buddha on up to contemporary spiritual authors.

An Insidious Intruder

Trying to eliminate ego has been kind of like a teeter-totter for me; just when I think I have it squashed, it pops up again out of nowhere. Over time, I have managed to reduce it to a weak and sickly thing that has only brief rallies of influence before it is sent back to bed.

I have been working to rid myself of ego for many years. It's a work in progress that I find quite liberating. It requires a lot of conscious effort and determination to extinguish ego, or more accurately to keep it at bay. By ego I mean a need for recognition, excessive pride, and a feeling of self-importance or superiority to others, and selfishness. I believe that the prevalence of ego in today's society is a consequence of materialistic values that appear to be the guiding principle of the majority these days.

As a young man, prior to embarking on my career, I was very humble and all about self-sacrifice and helping others. However, I remember an incident later in life that happened at a time when I was enjoying great success in my career. It illustrates how ego can unwittingly overshadow one's spirituality and disengage one from compassion for others.

I was walking down a city street with my son when he was 12 or 13 years old. We came upon a homeless man walking toward us. The man was dirty, in rags, weak and trembling. When we met, he did not speak but put his hand out for alms. I ignored him and shuffled my boy past.

My son stopped and grabbed my arm surprised at my lack of compassion. He insisted that I give him some money for the man, and he straight away gave it to him. I was mortified by my lack of compassion. The experience was a wakeup call.

It is difficult for me to admit to having had such a failure of character. I attribute it to ego as it happened during a time, I realize in retrospect, when my ego had a strong hold on me. The innocence and generosity of a child had shown me the deprivation of spirit that existed in me during that period of my life. It took a while, but thankfully, I managed to crawl out of the muck of ego, put on clean clothes, and reclaim my spirituality.

This taught me that ego is insidious; it gradually invades the psyche little by little so that one does not notice that it is happening. It can slowly become a more and more prominent part of one's personality and behavior. By the time your ego is full grown, you are not even aware of what a selfish and self-serving lump you have become.

Ego and the materialistic way of life go hand-in-hand. An inflated image of oneself is intimately intertwined with the selfishness, greed, and lack of compassion we see today. This is because ego is one of the motivators that drives us to try to seek recognition and prestige from the things we have, where we live, and the people with whom we associate.

I may be sticking my neck out here, but I do not think that recognition or prestige is a basic human need. I believe they are *created* needs from very effective marketing strategies that span decades. So many advertisements we see play to, or seek to create in us, a "need" for prestige or just being noticed whether it is for white teeth, a flashy car, a big house, or expensive clothes. We must find a way to resist and reclaim our humility and dignity.

How does ego conflict with becoming a more spiritual person? The egotist's primary concern is *their* needs. Consequently, ego can prevent us from seeing what those around us need. The sense of superiority that comes with ego can cause us to dismiss or overlook the adversity, suffering, and deprivation that others endure. This is one of the main ways that ego compromises expression of our spirit and militates against our becoming a spiritual person.

We are not defined or valued as individuals or human beings by what we have, how we look, or who our friends are. We are defined by the degree of humility we exhibit, how we live our lives, and how we treat other people; these are indicators of the degree to which we have become spiritual persons.

In fact, I believe that humility is an essential attribute of spiritual persons. I say this because humility indicates recognition that all that we are, the talents we have, and the friends, family, and possessions we have, came to us by the grace of God. Our humility is an expression of our gratitude for God's blessings large and small. I see humble people as having great strength, self-confidence, and restraint. They have a certainty that they are on the right path regardless of what others may think.

Chapter Four

What is the Nature of God?

Who or what is God? What is His most basic nature?

One could debate endlessly concerning whether or not He involves Himself in our individual lives, the progress of the human race, or whether He is loving, angry, forgiving, vengeful, etc. There are many opinions about these aspects and more, and support for each can be found in scriptures of various religions. Each of us must find our own "truth" concerning these attributes.

I have wondered about the nature of God at a more fundamental level. What might His primordial attributes be like and can they be expressed in language and images that we can understand?

After pondering the nature of God for some time, one day I sat down at my computer and the verse below flowed onto the screen. I must admit that it felt a little freaky reading it for the first time.

The All Powerful Unknowable

I am the Uncreated One.
I exist apart from the bounds of time.

I am beyond beginning and end
For I have always existed and always will.

I am both the Creator, and the created
For I made everything in heaven and Earth.

I cannot be created or destroyed.
I am everywhere and in all things.

I can transform myself into countless forms.
Yet, I am without form.

I am unknowable and unseen, but everywhere you look.

I am Love which is testimony to my existence!

As this verse illustrates, the qualities that we might imagine God or a higher being would have are to some extent a paradox, enigmatic, and most certainly beyond our limited awareness and understanding.

I am very open minded concerning spirituality, the nature of God, and the universe. I like to read a variety of sacred writings to expose myself to a wide variety of perspectives concerning religion, God, and how to live a spiritual life. For example, the Gnostic Gospels are quite interesting and anything but heretical as some religious believe.

I found the *Gospel of Mary Magdalene* to be especially fascinating because it had that very mysterious and other worldly tone not unlike the verse above. Moreover, it discussed aspects of spirituality not seen in any of the other Christian scriptures or gospels. Below is an excerpt from the *Gospel of Mary Magdalene* that I found to be very powerful and revealing about the fundamental nature of creation.

The first ten lines from the *Gospel of Mary Magdalene* that follow had an especially powerful effect on me. Here Mary is asking Jesus about the meaning and purpose of the physical world.

> [...] "What is matter?
> Will it last forever?"
>
> The Teacher answered:
> "All that is born, all that is created,
> all the elements of nature are interwoven and united with each other.
> All that is composed shall be decomposed; everything returns to its roots; matter returns to the origins of matter. Those who have ears, let them hear."

The six pages that preceded this passage are missing from the documents that were found in Egypt in 1896. Given this bit of discourse, one must wonder what revelations were revealed leading up to this declaration.

The basic ideas in these passages are not new to me, but my reaction to them was totally unexpected. When I read these lines in the gospel, it felt like primal memories buried deep in my soul came crashing forward revealing a fundamental, profound truth. The feelings were so powerful that I felt a little disoriented and confused by the effect they had on me.

These passages spoke to me on a very deep level. The words were both mysterious and wonderful. All of creation is interwoven and united—YES! All that is composed shall be decomposed—that is, all that is physical is transitory. Everything shall return to the Source (God).

We are drawn to the Source. It is a force of nature that transcends belief. It is that inexplicable yearning for meaning and purpose unique to the human condition. It is the search for our spirit-self and its birthplace.

❊   ❊   ❊

This next verse was written six months before the *All Powerful Unknowable*. It is another case where the words flowed effortlessly when I sat down to write. When this happens, I always wonder whether it was a product of my mind or if it was inspired by someone in the spirit world.

I am Spirit

I am Spirit.
I have existed before time began
and I will exist after the end of time.

I am you and you are Me.
I am a victim of doubt, skepticism, and ignorance.
I am present in bodies with minds that do not recognize Me.

I give you life—yet, you do not truly live.
I am love—yet, you do not share Me widely.

I am compassion—yet, you hide my light deep inside.
I am generous—yet, you do not give to those who are needy.

I give you knowledge, but you refuse to believe.

I show you the Path, but you turn away and choose another.

I provide good counsel, but you do not listen.

I am Spirit.
I am you, and you are Me.

One day you will awaken to Me
And our glorious light will shine upon the world!

The message here is clear: God lives within us. We must understand and believe that we exist as spirit, in conjunction with God, and not neglect or be afraid to express our divine qualities.

❁   ❁   ❁

Growing up in South Florida, I lived on a boat for several years as a child. What a wonderful life for a young boy! It was wonderful to be gently rocked to sleep at night by the waves.

Certain times of the year I would wake up to the sound of fish jumping and catch a few before heading off to school. Oftentimes, my brother and I would catch fish and crabs for dinner off the dock and bridge.

Ever since then, I have always had a great love and affinity for the ocean and water in general. In fact, for most of my adult life I have lived near the water. I returned to Florida almost thirty years ago and plan on staying for the rest of my life.

Now every morning while making breakfast I look out my kitchen windows upon the swimming pool in my backyard. I am often mesmerized by the waves and ripples moving across its surface and their interplay with rays of the sun. The beautiful blue water is always uplifting.

I found myself one day imagining that God might be like water since, under certain circumstances, it is so clear and pure as to be invisible, while at the same time very powerful. This next verse, is a product of my musing.

I Can Imagine...

I can imagine that God is like water...

I am certain that I see Him moving in the flow and swirls.

I feel Him all around gently embracing every part of me.

I am weightless in His arms as He buoys me up so that I keep site of the destination ahead.

He carries me when I am tired.

He is forgiving as I move through His ethereal essence.

Turbulent when His natural flow is resisted.

He slows my forward movement to assure my progress is deliberate and considered.

I am certain that I hear Him gently calling me to surrender to the natural flow that will take me home at last!

Each of us has our own beliefs concerning whether or not God exists, the nature of God, and what sort of characteristics He may have. Our natural tendency is to anthropomorphize Him and to attribute human emotions and motivations to what we believe to be His actions.

While this is understandable, I am of the belief that we have no clue concerning why things happen as they do. Our view is extremely narrow, finite, and largely limited to a physical existence. Whereas God's perspective is infinite and spans eternity.

We cannot begin to understand the reason for temporal occurrences without knowing God's long range plan for our individual and collective spiritual progression. Because of this, something that we see as tragic or bad for us in this life, may in fact be a necessary step for our long term spiritual evolution.

As many of us often say, "Everything happens for a reason." If we truly believe this, then we need to accept whatever happens with equanimity and have faith that it is all part of the plan and in our best interests on the scale of eternity.

I have given thought to this over the last few years in the face of what seems to be an inordinate number of disasters and tragedies around the world. The following are three essays I wrote between 2014 and 2015 searching for spiritual meaning in the face of the tragedies and calamities that were taking place. The articles are presented in the order in which they were written so that you can see the evolution of my thoughts concerning the potential positive outcomes of loss and catastrophe.

Calamity—A Test of Faith and Spirit

It seems that most people have faith that there *is* a God, but too little faith *in* God. Many people seem to believe that God does not play an active role in their life and that the adversities and calamities that we all must face are chance events.

I believe that life is a crucible of learning with the purpose of helping us to become aware of our spiritual existence beyond the physical plane, and to give us opportunities to express our spirit-selves. This purpose is too important to leave to chance, and without some guiding force, the learning would be too haphazard to allow for meaningful spiritual progression.

I believe that God has a life plan for each of us. The plan is perfect and designed to provide opportunities to learn and to express our spirit-selves. Everything that happens to us whether good or bad contributes to our spiritual growth. We lack the big picture and the long range view of eternity. Consequently, we may misinterpret an event in our lives as bad, when in the context of the larger scale of time past and future, it is actually good for us.

The sorrow we feel from the loss of a loved one serves a purpose. Loss of a job or destruction of our home provides an opportunity for us to reassess our priorities and how we live our life. Suddenly finding ourselves in financial ruin may help us appreciate the basic needs that God provides, and gives us new perspective on the destitute and impoverished. Through such hardships, our eyes (spirit) may be opened to new understanding, and compassion may spring forth raising us up from what unwittingly may have been a dark abyss of our prior existence.

But the true test of all of this is whether the lessons from calamity were truly learned, as evidenced by our actions going forward. After recovering, do we revert back to our previous way of living, or does the experience truly change the way we look at the world, life, and our fellow human beings, especially the poor and disenfranchised?

Even as we stand amongst the ruin of everything we held dear or in the face of loss of a loved one, we should give thanks for what God had given to us without any expectation or request for replacement of what was lost. This outlook was personified by a survivor of typhoon Haiyan in the Philippines in 2013 who had lost the little that he had. When asked by a reporter what he thought after seeing the massive destruction, he gave no complaint. Instead, he gave thanks for what was lost and for what was saved by simply saying, "Blessings, [God's] blessings."

The Transformative Nature of Tragedy

Traumatic events in our lives are usually the most transformative—whether it is nearly dying ourselves, the loss of a loved one, or some other calamity. It is sad that tragedy and heartbreak are often needed to initiate positive change in many of us.

These events may cause us to realize that we have been attracted to the neon lights of fame, fortune, and desire for far too long. We begin to see that the bright colors are artificial and without substance or spiritual quality. I believe that traumas can awaken us from a sleepwalk towards the spiritual desolation caused by a life driven by materialistic values rather than spiritual ones.

Tragedy often rekindles our compassion for others and expands our understanding of suffering. Traumatic events draw our spirit forth causing us to reach out to others, not so much to get support, as to give it. Not so much to grieve a loss, as to celebrate one life, and resolve to improve another (usually our own).

Our search for meaning in the loss of a loved one, more often than not, turns inward to seek how we can honor their memory, become better human beings, and truly live ourselves. These thoughts come, not so much from a fear of death, but rather to exalt life—to come to understand what is important in life, and in doing so, undergo a meaningful transformation for the better. The challenge is to integrate positive changes in us brought about by this transformation in a way that guides our lives continuously and irreversibly going forward.

Disasters: Nature or Providence?

Perhaps we all wonder at one time or another why major disasters occur where large numbers of people are killed or injured or there is large scale destruction of property. Is the motive force nature or providence? Some may say they are chance events or they result from natural processes. Still others (perhaps a minority these days) may say that they are acts of God.

Of course one cannot say with certainty who is right about why these things happen. If everything happens for a reason, then the big question is: *What is the reason?*

If we say that everything happens for a reason, then it implies that someone or something is behind and guiding events that happen in our lives, including major disasters. What value could a major disaster possibly have to humankind? To answer that question we must look at how disasters affect those directly impacted and how others not involved react.

Survivors may have lost loved ones and everything they own. They must find a way to cope and start their life all over again. These are major challenges to test one's inner strength, and for those who believe in God, one's faith that what happened was *somehow* in their best interest from the perspective of spiritual development.

For those directly affected, it is a terrifying, traumatic event. They will never forget the suffering that they had to endure, but more importantly, they will never forget the kindness and compassion of those who sought to help them in the aftermath. For some victims the help they receive is life-changing. That is, they make it a point to be kind and compassionate to others as they go forward with their lives.

But the reasons why disasters happen may go much further and beyond just those directly affected. I believe that large scale major disasters such as the tsunamis in Japan and Indonesia and other events are intended to have a transformative effect on the psyche of people around the world.

That is, such events are intended to make us reevaluate our values, how we live, our behavior, and how those contribute to the state of the world today. And having done that, strive to make positive changes in the way we live that are pleasing to God and that contribute to the creation of the better world we all want.

Such tragedies challenge our understanding of the purpose and meaning of life. Put another way, major traumatic events provide us with an opportunity for a spiritual awakening. Sadly, not all will be ready to hear the call, but many others will.

How the psyche of individuals may be affected by disaster will vary. We have seen from news accounts that many people are moved to a deep compassion for those directly impacted and those who can, flood into the area to help any way possible.

But we are all moved with great sorrow and compassion no matter where we are. What most of us do not realize is that the outflow of compassion triggered by the event is an expression of our divine selves that is showing us who we really are; who we are intended to be; and how we should live our lives everyday with or without disasters. I believe these are the things such events are meant to teach us.

So, are disasters good or bad? They are both. They bring great sadness, sorrow, and suffering for the loss of life, property, and basic needs. But they also bring to many a spiritual awakening and a new perspective on life and how we are meant to live. These events are intended to remind us that the material world is temporary while the human spirit is eternal and able to transcend all earthly circumstances.

If the foregoing makes sense or resonates with you, then it suggests that God does indeed try to guide us to greater expression of our higher, divine selves. So what is the fundamental nature of God? The answer lies within each of us, embedded in our personal life experiences and slowly revealed to us as our spiritual awareness grows.

✠   ✠   ✠

What place should God have in our everyday lives? I believe that we should make God a part of our every waking moment—a presence palpable. We should honor Him and pay homage to him throughout our day. We can do this in many ways. A very important one is for goodness to permeate our every thought and action. As exemplified by Jesus, working and living for good encompasses selflessness, a strong desire to help others whenever we can, and when needed, self-sacrifice to serve others before ourselves.

The attribute of goodness is a state of elevated spiritual being and connection with God. It is an expression of our spirit-selves. Inherent in (and requisite for) a life of goodness is compliance with God's commandments and mindfulness of His natural laws.

We also honor God by being present in the moments of our day so that we take notice of the beauty and wonders of nature all around us even in the most mundane setting. When we do this, we begin to see the beauty of God Himself, in that He *is*, and is *in* all things. On these occasions, our spirits soar toward the heavens, even if only for those few precious moments. We cannot help but yearn for more of such time on the wind.

I believe we and all life forms, even plants and bacteria, are a part of a spiritual collective that emanates from God. To hurt any member of the collective is to hurt ourselves and to hurt our creator. That is why we should cherish one another and all life.

While driving to work one day, the thought came to mind how all of the things I see around me are all wonderful and diverse expressions of God. Everywhere I turn, there he is: he is that tree over there, the bird on the light post, the flowers in the garden, the dog barking in the house next door, the raccoon in my trash can, and my neighbor washing his car.

Each and every one of his creations is exquisite in its detail, complexity, and beauty. God's creations have many facets or layers that can be revealed to us if we can cast away our self-imposed limitations, open our spirit as completely as possible, and allow the joy and wonder we had as children to come into play.

We need to look below the surface to where the true quality of all things resides. These thoughts gave renewed meaning to the idea that to truly love God is to love and cherish all living things, because all of these things are the many expressions of Him.

This world view sees all of the elements of creation as sacred. Seeing in this way is perhaps the most profound way we can give homage to God.

Chapter Five

How Do We Progress Spiritually?

The material world presents us with many challenges, not the least of which is maintaining awareness of our spiritual divinity and seeing opportunities for its expression. It's so easy to get caught up in the day-to-day of work and family.

Although these things and more can provide fertile ground for learning, many of us may not realize that God has certain expectations of us—laws to govern and guide life in the material world and when we return to the world of spirit. An extremely important one is the Law of Service. It is through actuation of this law in our lives that we express our spirit and evolve. I believe it to be a requirement for progression to higher spiritual planes.

How many people do you know who engage regularly in some form of service to others? In this day and age, it seems like many of us are too engrossed in our personal lives and the quest for fame, fortune, love, or whatever else to even think about helping others. As a consequence, we miss out on one of the most rewarding things in life—helping others through service.

The Law of Service is inherent in the commandments, "Thou shalt love thy neighbor as thyself" and "Thou shalt love the Lord thy God with all thy heart, and with all thy soul, and with all thy mind." In fact, if you believe that each of us is a part of God, then to love others is to love God and vice versa. Consequently, it could be said that the two commandments are simply different expressions of the same spiritual law.

We have a spiritual kinship with all of humanity. Therefore, people locally and around the world are our neighbors. We are expected to love them all, and in so doing, to provide service and help to anyone who needs it. As Silver Birch has said, the ability to provide unselfish service to others is essential to our spiritual progression and it is the single most important thing we can do to change the world.

❊ ❊ ❊

What if there were natural laws created by God that operate automatically in our daily lives to shape our behavior and lead us to a life of goodness? Cause and effect is a natural law that operates in the context of consequences for our actions, intentions, and behaviors. It often is mentioned in the series of books that contain the teachings of Silver Birch.

The spiritual principle of karma is another name for cause and effect. The concept of karma originated in ancient India and remains a central concept in Hinduism and Buddhism. The Law of Cause and Effect also is embodied by the biblical saying "You reap what you sow." Therefore, it is a spiritual law inherent in teachings of Judaism, Christianity, Islam, Buddhism, and Hinduism.

Cause and effect are thought to operate without the need for active participation of a deity. Although like the physical laws of the universe, I believe cause and effect were created and set into motion by God. In other words, the operation of the Law of Cause and Effect is automatic just like the laws of gravity.

Our thoughts/intentions and actions, both good and bad, have consequences that will automatically manifest. The effects may be immediate or delayed; obvious or subtle.

The basic principle is that the intentions and actions of an individual influence or determine how their life will play out going forward. Good intentions and a life of goodness (cause) will result in happiness and fulfillment (effect). Bad intent and bad behavior or actions will result in a life of suffering, frustration, and unhappiness. It is possible that bad karma may have negative effects on one's health due to the imbalance between spirit, mind, and body it creates.

While most people have a casual understanding of karma, many do not take it seriously as a principle that governs the quality of our lives. Something that few realize is that the spiritual principle of cause and effect is a powerful instrument that can be used to change our lives for the better. It provides the opportunity to break free from past bad behaviors and attitudes and the negative consequences (effects) they produce, and change our future.

Even as our karma plays out, we can decide what direction our life will take. Will we choose a fulfilling and happy life of goodness, love, and compassion, or a life of bitterness, jealousy, selfishness, greed, and hate devoid of any redeeming factors? Will we surrender to the darkness we have brought upon ourselves, or will we refuse to give up and instead emerge from the shadows and blaze a new path toward spiritual fulfillment?

The operation of cause and effect assures accountability and justice concerning all of our thoughts and actions. Based upon our intent and actions (cause), we produce the consequences that we may interpret as punishment or reward (effect). Bad actions or intent result in bad karma while good actions and intent create good karma. Thus, the Law of Cause and Effect encourages us to live a moral and ethical life to avoid bad consequences and unhappiness.

I hope that everyone can appreciate what a simple and perfect plan this is. The Law of Cause and Effect is the ultimate learning tool. Sadly, too few understand this. They go through life at various levels of misery and unhappiness without knowing that their behavior and the way they treat others is the cause of their suffering.

It is essential that we take personal responsibility for our actions and their consequences. Neither religious faith nor creed nor ritual or ceremony can remove the burdens we create for ourselves through our bad behavior. The burden can be reduced or removed only through reparation and striving to live a life of goodness and virtue going forward.

᯾ ᯾ ᯾

A Path from Darkness

…And Spirit told me, "Do not be consumed with fear and regret for past sins. Neither should your transgressions be dismissed nor forgotten. Rather, recognize them as lessons to be learned and do not repeat them. Use them to move forward and fuel your resolve to rise to higher levels of spiritual understanding and virtue."

Chapter Six

_____

God and Nature

Ancient and aboriginal people revered and even worshiped nature. We may look down on them as primitive but in fact they were intuitively spiritual with regard to nature. Modern man has to a great extent lost respect for nature as a force in its own right and for its nurturing qualities. The following essays remind us of how the natural places bring the joy and serenity that lift up our spirit, and if we are sufficiently spiritually aware, allow us to commune with God and His Holy Spirits.

Nature: A More Expansive Spirituality

When we go to beautiful wild places to get away from it all, it is sometimes difficult to describe what we feel. For me, it is an inexplicable feeling of belonging—a homecoming of sorts. It is a joyful feeling like I have met my soul mate. I want to linger endlessly and I lament when I must return to the steel and cement world.

This feeling of nature—the trees, animals, bugs, rocks, etc—as soul mate says something very profound. For those few hours, days, or however long in beautiful natural surroundings, we are on the threshold of awareness that we are a part of all of the earth and all living things that comprise nature. They are all a part of God and His divinity is a part of us and all things. As Jesus has told us in the *Gospel of Mary Magdalene*, "All that is born, all that is created, all the elements of nature are interwoven and united with each other."

Recognition of this truth has implications. One is that we are participating in an evolution of the earth and all life on it. We are but one species among millions on a trajectory of growth in consciousness and spiritual awareness. This knowledge carries with it great responsibility.

If all things are a part of God, then all things are sacred and demand our reverence, respect, compassion, and protection.

Although we may see humanity as superior to other forms of life, God may not share such an egocentric view. If that is the case, then other species may hold potential for development equal to us in God's eyes. It could be that they are just not as far along in their evolution as we.

Thomas Berry believed that God placed humanity *within* the natural order rather than above it. It is our arrogance as a species that sees itself as the one most pleasing in the eyes of God. Given the direction that humanity has taken in recent history, this may not be the case.

If God is everywhere and in all things, then exploitation and destruction of our planet and the life it holds are affronts to God. It is our arrogance in believing that our science and technology can master the forces of nature or improve on what God has created that has led to our current environmental, social, and spiritual crisis.

At the same time, I see a quiet, unobtrusive movement in progress. I see more and more people exhibiting various levels of spiritual enlightenment concerning the environment. I see small steps that help to reduce harm to the planet like buying organically grown foods, moving away from a meat-centered diet toward a more vegetarian diet, avoiding genetically modified food products (GMOs), greater sensitivity to animal rights, recycling, driving hybrid or electric cars, and so forth.

While these may seem like small things, they suggest a growing awareness of what has been discussed here. They are indications of the beginning of a step forward in spiritual evolution and awareness that will change the world in so many wonderful ways.

Sentinels of Peace

When I visited my daughter in Colorado last year, we went up to Lookout Mountain. What I really liked most about it was sitting under the trees while eating our lunch. It felt so welcoming and comforting. I could have sat there for hours and just listened to the breeze in the branches.

It was like a homecoming and having the love of family all around you. With all of the branches overhead and the tree trunks all around, I felt safe and protected. I had found sanctuary and tranquility. When it was time to go, my spirit protested, reluctant to leave a place of such beauty, serenity, and unconditional love.

Now the forest land beckons me once again. My heart yearns for reunion with my stalwart sentinels of peace.

Spirits Calling

Sometime after returning from my trip to Colorado, I was compelled to stop by a small grove of trees. As I looked up into the branches with flashes of the sun passing through on the breeze, I felt so much love. Love *for* the beautiful trees and love *from* the trees.

I felt a presence welcoming me to a meditation. It was a remarkably sublime feeling of calm, contentment, and fulfillment. It was a wonderful moment that I did not want to end.

I have walked past those trees many times before without noticing them. But this day I heard them call to me and say, "Come stay a while and let us commune with God and feel His love."

✼ ✼ ✼

If one is sufficiently present and spiritually aware, often we see ordinary things differently or notice and appreciate things others might overlook. There are wondrous and beautiful things all around us if only we would look through our spirit eyes.

The early morning often presents beauty that inspires me as reflected in the verses on following pages.

The Golden Morning

I love the golden morning light.
It's warm glow so beautiful.

And when it touches me
It feels so soft and satisfying,
Like a lover's caress.

I imagine that the hand of God is touching me.
That I am amidst His presence
And feeling His loving embrace.

As the golden morning turns to the brightness of a sun rising higher, my spirit rejoices and I am filled with joy!

The gentle warmth of the early hours has set the tenor of my day!

❀   ❀   ❀

Sometimes ordinary things we encounter in the course of our day can be a source of great inspiration, and if we stop to take notice and be really present in what we see before us, the spiritual revelation of *more* may be revealed to us.

Just So...

What is this heavenly radiance I see before me with such uncanny beauty?

It's like a sky full of stars, but it is morning.

The light emitted is bright, beautiful, wondrous, and other worldly.

I cannot take my eyes off the dazzling display
of what looks to be sparkling diamonds
and precious gems of all kinds
with fire like I have never seen before.

Hundreds of water droplets clinging to a screen
have caught the early morning light, just so...

Resulting in refraction of the light, just so...

Each droplet sparkles and pulsates with its own
unique color.

All shades and hues of a panoply of colors can
be seen more vivid and vibrant than I could have
ever imagined.

Is this how the universe of stars would look if the
dust and light years between us were removed?

Or is this the quality of light seen in the heavenly
realms?

But alas, the gentle morning sunbeams that gave
light, just so...

Impinging on ordinary droplets of water at an angle, just so...

Giving birth to such incredible beauty...

Must now give way to the sun's ascent and I am quickly transported back to Earth.

Exhilarated by what I have just seen,
I realize that there is so much more
beyond ordinary perception.

Another world of unimaginable wonders.
A revelation that was given, just so…

Conclusion

In the opening two sentences of his book *Anam Cara*, John O'Donohue said something very profound. He said, "It is strange to be here. The mystery never leaves you alone." It is indeed strange when we realize that we are spiritual beings cast into a physical world. We are out of our element. Upon birth we are immediately way out of our comfort zone.

It's no wonder so many people feel lost and confused and ask questions like, why am I here? What is my purpose? What gives my (earthly) life meaning? What should I be doing with my life? Thus, it's no surprise that we yearn for something more.

What you have read in this book reflects my personal grappling with these same questions. What I have shared with you represents the inspirations that provided many answers for me. I hope that it may have provided some for you also.

Perhaps the most important things my explorations and growing spiritual awareness have given me is a strong sense of what we are, how we are intended to live, and a somewhat mystical appreciation for the beauty of all things, including the mundane and obscure. We really do have two sets of eyes and two minds that create very different perspectives, experiences, and reactions to this strange world of the physical.

I have found that when we see ourselves as spiritual beings, strive to live a spiritual life, and express spiritual values in all that we do, the strangeness of being here is gone and we can feel comfortable, secure, and at home once again.

�֍   ✤   ✦

Appendix

Original Prayers

Prayer for Harmony

Dear God,

I strive to make myself whole, and by doing so come closer to you.

I wish to find the sacred harmony between spirit, mind, and body.

My only desire is to serve and honor you by expression of my spirit through acts of love and compassion.

I pray that my spirit may one day become attuned with, and radiate your divine love for all things.

Amen

Prayer for World Harmony

Lord God in Heaven,

I pray for peace, harmony, security, equality, and freedom for all of the children of Earth.

We long for the time when goodness and light will once again prevail over the evil and darkness which have ruled the earth for far too long.

I pray that your sacred light will continually grow ever brighter and purge the earth of all shadows and darkness where evil abides.

I ask that, where appropriate, your children come to understand that their salvation will not come through blind adherence to the doctrines and edicts of their religious faith.

But rather, simply by loving you and living a life of unselfish goodness and virtue.

May harmony between spirit, mind, and body found by one extend to the many and result in peace among nations and a spiritual renewal and awakening of the people of the world.

Lord hear my prayer!

An Expression of the Spirit

My dear God,

I ask for your guidance, and for the strength, determination, and courage to serve you to the best of my ability, at all times, without fail, in any manner you ask of me, without hesitation or fear.

My only desire is to serve and honor you by expression of my spirit through continual acts of love, compassion, and healing.

This is my heart's desire. This is who I am.
This is who I have always been and always will be.
This is my purpose in this life and the next.

Lord hear my prayer!

A Letter to God

Dear God,

I ask that through your grace and the efforts of your Holy Spirits that the dark minds of the wicked and selfish be turned toward the light of goodness, love, and compassion.

I ask that you give us world leaders and governments that are driven by a strong desire for the happiness, health, and well-being of their people and by a strong desire for a peaceful world.

I realize that transformation is a slow process and that sometimes it is only through great suffering that change takes place; that sometimes it is only through great injustice that justice can finally be achieved; that sometimes it is only through darkness that the search for light and truth begins.

It appears that you have set into motion circumstances to motivate us to change as individuals and as a civilization. You have pointed the way, but I understand that it is up to each of us to contribute to the creation of a better world for ourselves.

I pray with all my heart that the majority of us will hear your call and respond to adversity, not with anger, aggression, or grasping, but rather with equanimity and a strong desire to help one another get through the trials and tribulations we face, and to find lasting happiness through continuing acts of love and compassion.

I am, and forever will be, your devoted servant.

Other Books by the Author

*Building a Bridge Between Two Worlds.
Living the Life of Spirit* (2012)

Author's web sites:

www.livingthelifeofspirit.com

www.needforhealing.org

www.ingramcontent.com/pod-product-compliance
Lightning Source LLC
Chambersburg PA
CBHW020507030426
42337CB00011B/272